DATE

ROBERT OWEN
IN THE
UNITED STATES

AIMS HISTORICAL SERIES NO. 6

The American Institute for Marxist Studies (AIMS) is a non-profit educational, research and bibliographical institute. Its purposes are to encourage Marxist and radical scholarship in the United States and to help bring Marxist thought into the forum of reasonable debate to produce a meaningful dialogue among Marxist and non-Marxist scholars and writers. Its policy is to avoid sectarian and dogmatic thinking. It engages in no political activity and takes no stand on political questions. It grinds no axe for any group, party, sect, organization.

To these ends it invites the support and participation of all scholars and public-spirited individuals.

ROBERT OWEN
IN THE
UNITED STATES

OAKLEY C. JOHNSON

Foreword
by
A. L. Morton

Published for A.I.M.S. by
HUMANITIES PRESS
New York 1970

Printed in the United States of America

ACKNOWLEDGMENTS

Help was received from the following libraries and associations:

1. Library of Congress, General Reference and Bibliographical Division, Washington, D.C.
2. New York Public Library, Fifth Avenue & 42nd St., New York, N.Y.
3. State Historical Society of Wisconsin, Madison 6, Wisconsin. Benton H. Wilcox, Librarian.
4. Peabody Institute of the City of Baltimore, Baltimore 2, Md. Frank N. Jones, Director.
5. Public Library of Cincinnati & Hamilton County, Cincinnati 2, Ohio. Yeatman Anderson III, Curator of Rare Books.
6. University of Illinois Library, Urbana, Illinois. Miss Alma De Jordy, Photographic Reproduction Division.
7. Tamiment Institute Library, New York 3, N. Y. Mrs. Louise Heinze, Librarian.
8. Lenin Library, Moscow, USSR. Miss Bagrova, Chief of Department of Inquiry (Bibliographical and Informational), and Miss Frolova, Librarian.

      ✿   ✿   ✿   ✿

Thanks are due Robert Harris, formerly of the AIMS staff, for assistance in research and for stimulating suggestions; and to Dr. Herbert Aptheker, Director of AIMS, for encouragement and criticism.

                                          –O. C. J.

CONTENTS

FOREWORD

by A. L. Morton

Oakley C. Johnson has given an admirable account of the importance of Owen and Owenism in the development of progressive movements and thought in America: it may not be out of place to add a few words about the importance of America in the development of Owenism and the life story of Owen.

Owen went to America at a critical point of his life. After about 1820 he began to experience reverses in a career that had hitherto been one of uninterrupted success. His experiments at New Lanark had made him rich and famous, but he began to realise that the limits of what could be accomplished by such an undertaking within the restrictions imposed by the social structure of capitalism had been reached. Men could be made happier in such an environment, and their characters could be changed—but only up to a point. At the same time he found himself increasingly hampered by the prejudices of his partners. Owen could never be satisfied with anything less than complete success, and from this point his interest in New Lanark waned and he devoted progressively less of his energies to its management.

He turned, therefore, to attempts at establishing a Village of Co-operation on his fully socialist plan, where the limitations which had irked him at New Lanark would no longer operate. He tried first to enlist the support of the Government (and that the Government of Sidmouth and Castlereagh!), then of rich and influential backers. At every point he met with a polite interest which only concealed a profound indifference. As the nature of his projects became clearer this indifference hardened into hostility. Every attempt ended in failure.

These failures did not in the least persuade Owen that his plan was wrong—he was convinced to the last day of his life that it was right to the last dot and comma—but they did, I think, force him to conclude that England was not the place where a start could be made. And if not England, then where but in the U.S.A.?

As early as 1818 he had published a sympathetic account of the religious community of the Shakers which showed that America was already in his mind, and, indeed, at this time it seemed, not only to Owen but to thousands all over Europe, the natural site for every kind of social experiment. It was a *new* world, whose people had left behind them, when they crossed the Ocean, many of the worst features of the old. It was a world without kings and aristocrats, of civil and religious liberty, a world that, from a distance at least, and if one could shut one's eyes to the evil of slavery, seemed to offer something like equality of opportunity to all comers. And its Revolution, less than fifty years old, had established the first and as yet the only full political democracy in the world. Owen was aware enough of the limitations of political democracy and in Britain had always refused to concern himself with it. But in the *Discourses* printed in this volume he shows a realisation that, with all its limitations, American democracy offered possibilities that existed nowhere else. In these *Discourses* we can see a confidence and a sense of opportunity that none of his previous writings had displayed.

There were practical reasons, also, for the choice of America, and, in his most visionary moments Owen still remained the shrewd man of affairs who had made such a success at New Lanark. America was a vast territory still barely populated. Land was there for the taking, or, at least, fantastically cheap. At Harmony he was able to buy from the Rappites for £30,000 a property whose equivalent he could not have found anywhere in Britain for ten times that sum. Owen was a rich man as industrialists went in those days but he knew that his private fortune would have been quite inadequate to realise his plan anywhere in the Old World.

Yet it was probably the less tangible inducements which attracted him most, the conviction that here alone the mental independence which was for him the foundation stone of his plan could be quickly and completely won. And he must have realised that because America was for so many the promised land of freedom and equality it was there that he could best hope to attract men and women of the quality which his plan demanded. In this he was certainly right: while New Harmony had its share of idle talkers it had, as Johnson so well shows, more than its share of outstanding talent and dedicated idealism.

I think, therefore, that Owen came to America at this point of his life as the almost inevitable consequence of the dead end which his efforts seemed to have reached in Britain. Yet once more, though New Harmony accomplished many things and brought such rich gifts to the U.S.A., for Owen it proved another failure that left him a poor

man and forced him to begin all over again. Paradoxically it was this
failure that led to the most important and fruitful step in Owen's
whole career.

During his absence in America a broad movement had grown
among the [British] workers on the basis of his teachings. It was to
these workers that he now turned. They were not the public he would
have chosen. His greatest weakness was always his inability to see
in the workers a positive historical force, and, as his references to his
New Lanark employees in the first of these *Discourses* show, he always
felt that a wide gulf existed between him and them. To the end of
his life he remained impatient of the piecemeal enterprises of these
artisan cooperators. Nevertheless, here was a body of men prepared to
listen to him, and not only to listen but to work and make sacrifices
for the cause he and they believed in.

So for the first time, socialism left the study and came into the
streets, the workshops and the trade union branches. It took a hold
upon the minds of working men and women which was never hereafter to be wholly broken and which has led stage by stage to our
modern world movement for the emancipation of the masses. This,
though he never fully understood it, was to be Owen's greatest achievement, and the reason why we treasure and study his deeds and writings
today. And it was in a very real sense the failure of his American
venture, upon which his highest hopes had been set, which led him
to this new stage.

For this reason, if no other, I would welcome the publication of
these almost forgotten documents, though, in truth, they are note-
worthy for themselves. In none of his writings is his thought bolder,
clearer and more confident, in none is his faith in the possibilities
latent in mankind more apparent.

And they are a record of a period in the history of socialism which,
for all its incidental extravagances, is marked by a warmth and a
generosity, a spring-like promise. It was a time when a new hope of
a better world was growing in men's hearts, a time when nothing
seemed impossible. These hopes may not have been immediately
fulfilled: history has proved that in the long run they were abundantly
justified.

For this reason I should like to quote in conclusion a delightful
characterisation of Owen by an American utopian, Adin Ballou, the
founder of the Hopedale Community, which breathes the very spirit
of those years of promise.

"In years," he wrote, "nearly seventy-five; in knowledge and experience superabundant; in benevolence transcendental; in honesty without disguise; in philanthropy unlimited; in religion a sceptic; in metaphysics a Necessitarian Circumstantialist; in morals a universal excursionist; in general conduct a philosophical non-resistant; in socialism a Communist; in hope a terrestial elysianist; in practical business a methodist; in deportment an unequivocal gentleman."

—A. L. MORTON

ROBERT OWEN
IN THE
UNITED STATES

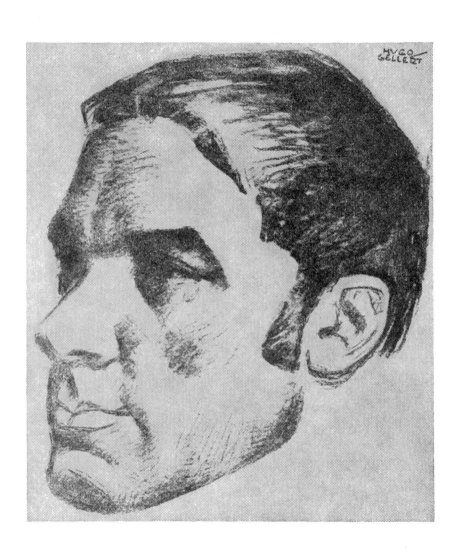

INTRODUCTION

By

Oakley C. Johnson

Publication in book form of Robert Owen's two *Addresses* to Congress in 1825 and his Fourth of July *Oration* in New Harmony, Indiana in 1826 has waited almost a century and a half; the historical consequence of their author is, of course, universally acknowledged and now readers may test for themselves the relevance of these particular products of his remarkable mind.

The *Addresses* were delivered during Owen's first visit to the United States, which extended from late 1824 to mid-1825; the *Oration* during his second visit, from late 1825 to mid-1827. He made two additional visits to this country.

The contemporary significance of Owen is reflected in the resurgence of a literature concerning him; examples are: *The Angel and the Serpent* (1964) by Professor William E. Wilson of Indiana University, and *My Indiana* (1964) by Irving Leibowitz; the issuance in 1966 of the third edition of G. D. H. Cole's *Life of Robert Owen;* and also in 1966 the publishing of a new edition of the 1945 volume, *Angel in the Forest* by Marguerite Young; the republication in two volumes (1966, 1968) of Owen's autobiography; and, in 1968, the publication by Teacher's College of Columbia University of J. F. C. Harrison's *Utopianism and Education: Robert Owen and the Owenites.*

Not unimportant, furthermore, from the point of view of Owen's rating in this country, is the fact that on August 21, 1965, Stewart L. Udall, then United States Secretary of the Interior, officially presented a National Landmarks Plaque to the State of Indiana at New Harmony, in honor of what Robert Owen and his co-workers had done. It has become a matter of national as well as local pride that a socialist community was once set up there.

The *Addresses* and *Oration* comprise two major—but neglected— reflections of Owen's efforts and concepts. That they are neglected becomes apparent when one examines, for instance, A. L. Morton's *The Life and Ideas of Robert Owen,* probably the best all-round treatment of Owen and Owenism in existence. For, despite the relative

1

completeness of this work, Morton made but little mention of Owen in America, and did not list the present *Addresses* and the *Oration* in his bibliography. The American Institute for Marxist Studies, which is sponsoring this book, has thus restored to history three important items of Owen's literary remains.

The reason for Morton's overlooking these American works lies doubtless in the fact that none of them has been republished in full for more than a century, though referred to often enough. The two *Addresses* to Congress were gotten out as a pamphlet during Owen's lifetime, and the Fourth of July *Oration* appeared immediately after delivery in the *New Harmony Gazette*, the community's own newspaper. But since then they have not appeared in print anywhere, even in the admirable *Backwoods Utopias* (1950) by Arthur Eugene Bestor, Jr., which, up to the present, contains the most thorough American research on Owen.

This situation led to some difficulty in the search for the *text* of the speeches. On September 11, 1962, the Library of Congress reported that the *Addresses* were "too brittle to film," and on June 29, 1964, the same Library said the *Oration* was "missing in inventory." Thanks to the Peabody Library in Baltimore and the State Historical Society Library of Wisconsin, the texts were nevertheless found, and photocopies made. A few more years neglect might have made their recovery impossible.*

The publication of these speeches in observance of the anniversaries of their delivery is especially proper because of the two-fold *Owenite legacy* that is now affirmed in all writings about the community he tried to found. Owen's experiment in socialism failed, says Leibowitz, but, "What New Harmony gave Indiana, the United States and the world is precious and important." Leibowitz had in mind the amazing cultural heritage of that experiment. He—as well as Wilson and Bestor and Udall—recounts how the "boatload of knowledge" that Owen brought down the Wabash River to New Harmony carried the foremost educators and scientists of the time. Among them were William Maclure, a Scottish scientist and promoter of Pestalozzi's educational theories; Thomas Say, a zoologist; Charles Alexander Lesueur, a French

---

*Not long before publication, the present editor discovered a copy of Owen's *Two Addresses* stowed away in a Pamphlet Volume in the New York Public Library, bound with other pamphlets. The Library has now transferred this item to the Rare Book Collection and re-numbered it, which is a distinct service to admirers of Robert Owen.

artist and naturalist; Dr. Gerard Troost, a Dutch geologist; Constantine Rafinesque, an ichthyologist; Dr. Joseph Neef, a Swiss educator; also Madame Marie D. Fretageot, a teacher of girls, and her co-worker, Phiquepal d'Arusmont, a teacher of boys.

In his tribute to the founder of New Harmony, Secretary Udall said: "After contributing four-fifths of his personal fortune to this experiment, Owen withdrew from the Community and gave shares to those who wished to remain and carry it forward. In many ways called a failure, one can only say today, with hindsight: would that we had more such ventures in our history."

So notable were these co-workers of Robert Owen—brought together by him to make socialist New Harmony shine the more—that the Indiana Academy of Science hailed them, May 12-14, 1927, on the occasion of the Centennial Anniversary of Western Science, held in New Harmony where, according to the *Proceedings* for that date, "scientific investigation in that region practically began." A paper presented there by David Starr Jordan of Stanford University and Amos W. Butler of Indianapolis concludes thus: "For more and more, New Harmony is becoming a place of pilgrimage for the social scientist, the educator, the historian, the student of the natural and of the physical sciences and the tourist. A beaten pathway has been made to the door of New Harmony."

As a result of this emphasis on education and science, New Harmony succeeded in chalking up a catalog of "firsts" in American cultural history. These included the first infant school, the first kindergarten, the first trade school, and the first adult education classes; also the first woman's club (Fanny Wright's Female Social Society, 1825). The equality of women with men was an accepted principle at New Harmony, as were free public schools and free public libraries.

But this is only half of the direct Owenite legacy. There must also be considered Owen's own family, his four sons and one of his three daughters, who came with him to New Harmony and remained, becoming citizens of the United States and notable leaders in it. The oldest son, Robert Dale Owen, became a congressman, a valued contributor to the *Atlantic Monthly*, an opponent of slavery and a champion of the rights of women. According to Secretary of the Treasury, Salmon P. Chase,[1] it was a letter from Robert Dale Owen, more than any other one thing, that influenced Abraham Lincoln to

---

1. Irving Leibowitz, *My Indiana*, p. 279. See also Marguerite Young, *Angel in the Forest*, p. 314.

issue the Emancipation Proclamation. While in Congress, Robert Dale Owen introduced and won the passage of a bill establishing the Smithsonian Institution, our first government-sponsorship of science. One further point about him:[2] The *Documentary History of American Industrial Society* by Commons and Associates, Vol. V, has as frontispiece a portrait of Robert Dale Owen, captioned "Leader of the Working Men's Party in New York, 1829-1830." These were the years that the world's second political labor party ran candidates for public office (the first being in Philadelphia, 1828).

David Dale Owen became a geologist, and was in fact the first official United States Geologist. "The U. S. Geological Survey," said Secretary Udall, in the address referred to, "owes an immeasurable debt to this gentle, scientific scholar." David Dale Owen married one of the two daughters of Dr. Joseph Neef in the "boatload of knowledge."

Richard Owen, also a geologist, became professor of natural science at Indiana University, and the husband of Dr. Neef's other daughter. The third son, William Owen, business manager of New Harmony and one of its leaders, unfortunately died in mid-career; but he was founder of the Thespian Society, which, says Professor Wilson, "gave a vitality to the theatre in New Harmony that lasted almost a hundred years. Jane Dale Owen, Robert Owen's daughter, married Robert H. Fauntleroy, astronomer and meteorologist.

New Harmony was important for its ordinary citizens, too—those who were *not* scientific geniuses and *not* children of Robert Owen. Without attempting to follow through on this thought, I will simply mention one couple residing in the community who named their infant son Hugh OWEN Pentecost. Years later Hugh O. Pentecost, a liberal minister in a New Jersey church, defended the cause of the martyred Haymarket labor leaders headed by Albert R. Parsons, and was forthwith ejected from his pastorate. Pentecost then entered the profession of law and, as a side issue, conducted lectures in New York City, where, among other innovations, he provided a forum for such notable dissenters as the young high school student, Elizabeth Gurley Flynn. I am indebted for this item to Mrs. Bertha W. Howe,**

2. *Documentary History of American Industrial Society*, (Vol. V, by J. R. Commons and Helen L. Sumner).

**Mrs. Bertha W. Howe is the subject of an AIMS-sponsored publication: *An American Century: The Recollections of Bertha W. Howe, 1866-1966*. Humanities Press, New York. 1966. Oakley C. Johnson, editor.

who herself in 1902-1903 took down many of Pentecost's lectures in shorthand and had them published in *The Truth Seeker* (1873-1912).

In thinking of New Harmony's contribution to American education, we must, of course, remember particularly Robert Owen's initiative in the field of schooling at his textile factory in New Lanark, back in Scotland; also his disapproval of corporal punishment as a pedagogical method, which he forbade in his school there. So impressive and original was Owen's work in the training of children that Karl Marx was moved to say the following: "From the Factory System budded, as Robert Owen has shown in detail, the germ of the education of the future, an education that will, in the case of every child over a given age, combine productive labor with instruction and gymnastic, not only as one of the methods of adding to the efficiency of production, but as the only method of producing fully developed human beings."[3]

In view of this comment by Marx, Professor Harrison's statement in his *Utopianism and Education: Owenism and the Owenites,* is pertinent: "There was a breadth in the Owenite religious and social opinion of the early nineteenth century, and the reaction to it was therefore hostile and scornful. Perhaps Owen was correct when he diagnosed: 'I am termed a visionary only because my principles have originated in experience too comprehensive for the limited locality in which people have hitherto been interested.'" (p. 38)

Simultaneously Owen carried on a long, determined struggle in England to reduce child labor, the deadly enemy of the education of children. "Children at this time," he wrote, when he was trying to get Parliament to adopt his Bill to regulate the labor of children, "were admitted into the cotton, wool, flax and silk mills, at six and even at five years of age. The time of working, winter and summer, was unlimited by law, but usually it was fourteen hours per day, — in some fifteen, and even, by the most unhuman and avaricious, sixteen hours."

His description in early writings of these inhuman factory conditions inspired Lewis Mumford to say, in *The Story of Utopias*: "I do not speak too harshly of the early industrial age; it is impossible to speak too harshly. Take the trouble to read Robert Owen's *Essay on the Formation of Character* (Manchester: 1837) and learn what conditions were like in a model factory run by an enlightened employer: it is a picture of unmitigated brutality."

---

3. *Capital,* Vol. I, International Publishers edition, 1947, p. 489. Engels quoted this identical passage in *Anti-Dühring,* International Publishers edition, 1934, p. 353.

The opposition that Owen met from other employers and from officials when he tried to get even the most elementary reforms through Parliament led him to think about the possibility of communist settlements in the United States, a new country free from feudal hangovers, possessed of a republican form of government, and blessed with available land.

Others had the same idea, and, as is well-known, scores of socialist communities—including famed Brook Farm—were set up in various parts of the United States before, during and after the existence of Owen's community. "Not a reading man but has a draft of a new community in his waistcoat pocket," mused Ralph Waldo Emerson. New Harmony, however, was the first important secular socialist community in this country. The earlier settlements holding property in common were religious. New Harmony started in 1824, Brook Farm in 1841.

Mention of Brook Farm brings up the thought of the other utopian socialists, Francois Charles Fourier (1772-1837) and Claude Henri de Saint-Simon (1760-1825), both of France, who also had a strong influence on the United States. Orestes Brownson, editor of the Boston *Quarterly Review* and author of *The Laboring Classes,* was a disciple of Saint-Simon. Albert Brisbane, a contributor to Horace Greeley's New York *Tribune,* and author of *Social Destiny of Man,* was—like Greeley himself—a follower of Fourier. Parke Godwin, son-in-law and biographer of William Cullen Bryant, was a Fourierist, and produced the important work, *Democracy, Constructive and Pacific.* The Rev. George Ripley, Congregational pastor and Fourierist, was organizer of Brook Farm, which was joined by—among others—the novelist, Nathaniel Hawthorne. These utopian efforts, coming fifteen years after Owen's *Addresses* to Congress, were important threads in United States history.

The question arises: Why did the idea of socialism awake such a broad and enthusiastic response in the America of 1825-1840, in and out of Congress?

This deserves extensive study, but we can include here only a few thoughts, suggested by Bestor, Commons, Foner, and other specialists in labor history. Among other things, conditions in early capitalist America were far from ideal. Nor was the future at that time reassuring in all respects to thinking men. Many were horrified by the reckless individualism let loose by the Industrial Revolution, and apprehensive about what lay ahead. There was a felt need to find remedies for evils already visible here in the new world, and to overcome greater dangers that threatened.[4]

One of these thinking men was Langdon Byllesby, who authored *Observations on the Sources and Effects of Unequal Wealth* (New York, 1826). Byllesby wanted to avoid violence in solving the problems of unequal wealth, and, hunting around for a method of "peaceful reform," he seized on some of Owen's theories as a possible way out. So, "with the aid of the bright light shed on it by that distinguished Philanthropist, Mr. Robert Owen, and his coadjutors," Byllesby reflected that the most likely method would be to give to each person the full product of his labor, and have cooperation of each with all. Byllesby was not as single-minded nor as clear as Owen, but it is interesting that he saw rich-against-poor as the basic problem, and, to a limited extent, Owen's *socialism* as the basic solution.[5]

In that fluid period between handicraft production and rising industrial capitalism, it was easier, perhaps, to ponder on new social directions than it was later, after the capitalist mode of production became set and established in people's minds.

Owen's experiment at New Harmony failed, as did all the others. He lost the bulk of his fortune of a quarter of a million dollars in trying to make socialism work. There has been much speculation on *why* the venture failed, and, generally, Owen has been blamed as *impractical*, socialism as *impracticable*. But the central truth was pointed out years ago by Frederick Engels, who said that "The Utopians . . . were utopians because they could be nothing else at a time when capitalist production was as yet so little developed."[6]

To call a man "impractical" who was able to become one of the richest men of his time, who mastered and improved the business and factory techniques of an entire industry, is obviously an inadequate explanation. The fact that he perceived the inhuman and inhumane aspects of capitalist manufacture suggests he was far superior to his fellow businessmen. Engels described Owen as "a man of almost sublimely childlike simplicity of character and at the same time a born leader of men such as is rarely seen."[7] Owen tried to establish communism as he conceived it, in a community, as an example to the world; at the same time he strove also to bring about such reforms

---

4. Bestor, *Backwoods Utopias*, pp. 97 ff.

5. Leon Joseph Blau, *Social Theories of Jacksonian Democracy*, 1947, pp. 343 ff.

6. Frederick Engels, *Anti-Duhring*, International Publishers, N. Y., 1934, p. 292.

7. *Ibid.*, pp. 287-288.

as a shorter working day and a limitation of child labor. He was "practical" in this sense, that he sought to *practice* humanism.

Modern critics of Owen and of New Harmony have concentrated overmuch on minor shortcomings, on deficiencies that need not be, and are not, denied. There were too many people at New Harmony, there were not enough skilled craftsmen, there were gaps between theory and practice, there were mistakes. The community-of-property plan had to be given up after only four years, and Owen died a poor man.

But there were positive historical accomplishments, some of which have been stated. There was the larger philosophical accomplishment of helping to open the path for Marxist thought, which A. L. Morton has demonstrated so ably. Any man who does as well with his life as Robert Owen, has not done badly.

It should not be thought a calamity that there were "Utopians" in the days of Sir Thomas More and Francis Bacon, or Francois Charles Fourier and Robert Owen. It was a tribute to Man's dauntless idealism which rises like a flower despite surrounding murk and muck. It has been said that "A map of the world that does not include Utopia is not worth glancing at." The utopians, such as Edward Bellamy, who did not plan actual socialist colonies enriched literature with stories of ideal societies.

Owen arrived in the United States, as stated, in late 1824, preceded by his reputation as a notable social reformer, and armed with letters of introduction to many leading Americans. He set himself, it appears, two tasks: to meet and if possible to convince government leaders of the value of his *plan* to reform society; and to purchase a tract of land where a demonstration of the *plan* could be staged. He wanted influential converts, and a living social laboratory.

He carried out both tasks. He met presidents and law-makers, and he bought the town of Harmony, where the Rappite religious community had already been flourishing for ten years, changing its name to *New* Harmony. The circumstances were outwardly propitious, and the laboratory was made to order. At the beginning of 1825, he interrupted his work in New Harmony to go to Washington, D.C., to *negotiate*—this is not too strong a word, considering Owen's intention—with the United States government about socialism.

Owen addressed Congress twice in 1825, the first time on February 25, the second on March 7. The first speech was arranged by

Henry Clay, Speaker of the House of Representatives; the second, by the incoming President, John Quincy Adams, who had heard the first. The speeches were delivered in the Hall of Representatives before a joint session of Congress, attended also by Justices of the Supreme Court, members of the Cabinet, and Adams' predecessor, James Monroe.[8]

At this time Owen visited Thomas Jefferson at Monticello and James Madison at Montpelier. The next year Jefferson spoke of Owen in a letter (Aug. 7, 1825) to the abolitionist and woman's rights advocate, Frances Wright, concerning her proposed Nashoba community for freed Negroes, patterned after New Harmony. Jefferson wrote: "It [her idea] has succeeded with certain of our white brethren, under the care of a Rapp and an Owen; and why may it not succeed with the man of color?"[9]

The press, says Arthur Eugene Bestor, Jr., gave Owen's speeches the same prominence as it gave Adams' *Inaugural Address*. The Washington, D.C., *National Intelligencer* (March 1), for instance, gave the entire second page to the full text of Owen's first lecture, and, on March 15, gave identical treatment to the second one. The Richmond *Enquirer* (March 11), commenting on the second speech, noted that though Owen spoke for nearly three hours, "he was listened to with great attention and respect." The *Daily National Journal* of Washington, D.C., (March 1) commented: "The propositions are remarkable for their boldness and novelty, and if the deductions are not always conclusive, they are plausible and ingenious." Says Bestor, summing up the contemporary reaction: "To a surprising extent the American press conceded the economic feasibility of Owen's plan in the abstract, and questioned only its relevance to American conditions."

Not all the comment was favorable. Many questioned whether Americans could accept Owen's plan, since they "are naturally ambitious and impatient of restraint." The *Daily National Journal* quoted above was obliged to say, "we are a little sceptical as to the probability of any moral power being applied to circumstances which so change their character and course" as to bring such a society into being. As time went on, the religious issue became dominant among critics.

---

8. Bestor, *Backwoods Utopias*, pp. 11 ff.
9. *The Writings of Thomas Jefferson*, edited by Paul Leicester Ford, Vol. X, p. 344 (G. P. Putnam's Sons, New York, 1892-1899).

Owen was opposed and assailed, not because of his *socialist*, but his *atheist* views.

Owen had affirmed his anti-religious opinions many years earlier in England. Now, in the New World, and a year after his appearance before Congress, he took occasion to deliver the Fourth of July *Oration* included here. In this "Declaration of Mental Independence" he went further than he ever had previously, listing Religion, Private Property, and Marriage (in its religio-property aspect) as the trinity of evils which held back Man's progress. This was the most iconoclastic point of his career, the peak of his revolutionary progress.

The three works are excellent specimens of his style and thought, and they illustrate—if one can also imagine the actual presence of Owen's intense and earnest personality—how he was able to persuade and enthuse great numbers of people in the cause of human betterment.

In his first *Address* to Congress, Owen emphasizes the magnitude of the social change he contemplates, one "greater than all the changes which have hitherto occurred in the affairs of mankind." It is to be a change which will abolish "ignorance and poverty" and "secure happiness to every individual." A change, further, that will benefit not only the people of the United States but those of the West Indies, Canada, South America, and, ultimately, the old world. In short, he calls upon his distinguished auditors, "the rulers of these states," to decide "the destinies of the human race."

Such is his unshakable belief in the importance of the experiments which, he says, "I commenced more than twenty-five years ago, at New Lanark, in Scotland," experiments which were made "for the benefit of mankind."

He does not minimize the moral and social basis of his plans. On the contrary, these are his reasons for advancing them, and he expects his hearers to understand and approve this humanist basis.

Owen sets forth not only the humanitarian, but also the economic aspect of his proposal: that *every* individual should *always* be able to get "a full supply of those things which are necessary and the most beneficial for human nature," a condition which would require that people be united under "a social system" that would guarantee such benefits. He would have us become "a new people, having but one common interest."

This first speech was thus chiefly hortatory, rather than planful. "The Government and Congress of this new empire have only now . . .

to will this change," he declared, "and it will be at once effected." The crux of his point was clear: "In the new system, union and cooperation will supersede individual interest," he said, and: "The inumerable and incalculable evils and absurdities which have arisen from the inequality of wealth will be effectively overcome and avoided throughout all the future."

In his second *Address,* Owen proceeds to explain some of the details of his "new system of society." In doing this he recalls what was done at New Lanark, and reads extracts from his previous works. He stresses the need for the proper training and education of the young, and for "charity, benevolence, and kindness," which he describes as "genuine" or "rational" religion.

He then proceeds to describe the arrangement and working of the buildings and lands of his model community. He announces that he has purchased the settlement of Harmony, on the Wabash, in Indiana, and declares: "I mean to carry these measures of amelioration to the full extent of my means and influence, into immediate execution." It is to be a society of "union, cooperation and common property," where would exist "genuine liberty and equality."

It is useful here to take note of later writings of Owen on American soil, written during other visits here, of which selected letters and articles were included by Professor John R. Commons in Vol. VII of the *Documentary History of American Industrial Society.* The frontispiece of this volume is a portrait of Robert Owen, captioned, "Father of Industrial Communism in America." Two of these quoted papers which Owen wrote are: "An Address to the Inhabitants of the United States of North America" (New York *Herald,* Sept. 21, 1844); and "To the Capitalists and Men of Extensive Practical Experience in New York" (New York *Daily Tribune,* April 2, 1845).

In the second of these occurs the notable passage, in which he seeks to win rich men over to his socialist proposals:

"These establishments will enable the capitalists and men of extensive practical experience to solve without difficulty the Great Problem of the Age, that is, how to apply the enormous and ever-growing new scientific powers for producing wealth, beneficially for the entire population, instead of allowing them to continue, as heretofore, most injuriously to create enormous riches for the few and to impoverish the many, driving them toward a desperation that will ultimately, if not untimely [sic] prevented by this measure, involve the over-wealthy in utter destruction."[10]

Owen's third and fourth visits to America were eventful in several other respects. The third saw his great 8-day public debate in Cincinnati (1829) on the subject of religion, in which the Rev. Alexander Campbell defended Christianity. The fourth saw his meeting with Ralph Waldo Emerson who described him as "the most amiable, sanguine, and candid of men." Emerson declined to support Owen's ideas, but he said: "And truly I honor the generous ideas of the Socialists, the magnificence of their theories, and the enthusiasm with which they have been urged."[11]

Thanks to the recent researches of Professor Robert C. Reinders of Tulane University, our knowledge of the extent of Owen's influence in this country has been broadened considerably. It is known that Owen went to New Orleans during his third American visit, and even threw out a challenge "to the Clergy" in the *New Orleans Argus* of January 29, 1828. Going beyond this, Professor Reinders has unearthed a New Orleanian, Judge T. Wharton Collens (1812-1879), a Roman Catholic, who was something of a convert to Owen's socialism, though not to his irreligion. Collens developed his own type of socialism, wrote an allegory entitled *Eden of Labor: or the Christian Utopia,* and, amazingly, cooperated with two northern Christian Socialists, Edward H. Rogers, a Methodist, and Jesse H. Jones, a Congregationalist, in propagating their common ideas for social betterment.

In a broad evaluation of Owen, it is a little difficult sometimes—but necessary—to avoid hero-worship. He was not alone in coming to the thought of some kind of cooperative social re-organization. Further, as scholarly research has shown, he had big and little shortcomings—such as his concentration on a vision to the exclusion of attention to immediate problems, and his later interest in spiritualism despite his renunciation of religious beliefs. He was far from having a complete, classical education.

Yet we must affirm that his personal reforming power was notable, and that he was and remains a symbol of something great in the history of thought.

---

10. Commons, *Documentary History of American Industrial Society,* Vol. VII, p. 166.

11. Ralph Waldo Emerson, *Complete Works,* edited by Edward Waldo Emerson, Vol. X, pp. 326-327 (Houghton Mifflin Co., Boston, New York, 1903-1932).

Perhaps attention should be paid to the contributions of Owen's associates, such as William Maclure, a fellow Scotsman and also a rich man, who gave his attention and support to advanced theories of education. He was a member of Owen's "Boatload of Knowledge." Bestor rates him as superior to Owen in certain respects: Maclure, for example, did not minimize class conflict, as did Owen. According to Bestor, Maclure insisted that "none but the millions can benefit the millions."[12]

I cannot conclude this brief discussion of Owen's views without adverting to a mistaken conclusion drawn by Professor William E. Wilson in *The Angel and the Serpent*, a book previously referred to. In speaking of Owen's visit to the British colony of Jamaica, where Negro slavery existed (p. 164), he says the following: "With all his humanitarianism, slavery never seemed evil to Owen; equality, as he defined it, did not include equality of the races." Again (p. 118), he says: "Robert Owen's concept of social equality did not extend to 'persons of color.'" Still again (p. 196), in praising Robert Dale Owen for his opposition to slavery, Wilson asserts that "his father, Robert Owen, with all his fervid humanitarianism, was stone-blind to the evils of slavery and saw no place for Negroes in a community of equality."

These assertions are simply untrue. The truth is that Robert Dale Owen learned his humanitarianism from Robert Owen, his father. So did Frances Wright, the founder of the Owenite community at Nashoba, Tennessee, referred to previously. So did Owen's daughter, Jane Dale Owen, who began her lecture on "The Principles of Natural Education" by calling for education for "the whole human race." (*Owenism and Education*, p. 176.) So did the Owenite, William Thompson, who, in advocating the "free development" of every child, wrote (*Owenism and Education*, p. 221): "In Miss Frances Wright's amiable and spirited exposition of the principles of her co-operative establishment at Nashoba, Tennessee, on the east bank of the Mississippi, in conjunction with General La Fayette and some other enlightened individuals, for educating and improving the blacks equally with the whites, this guarantee of mental liberty is given."

Robert Owen himself in his "New View of Society," declared it "admits neither of exclusion nor of limitation," and in his "Institution

---

12. Bestor, *Backwoods Utopias*, p. 150.

for the Formation of Character" he invited "all the nations of the world—men of every colour and climate."

Owen hoped that the rich would generously lead the way to socialism, and was convinced that the workers could not rise of themselves—two notions that applied also to his attitude toward blacks. Herein lay his weakness.

Wilson's over-hasty and superficial generalization mars an otherwise useful book on Owenite history.

Owen was born in Newtown, Wales, May 14, 1771, and went to London to work at the age of 10. By the time he was 20 he was manager of one of the largest cotton mills in Manchester, and became manager of the New Lanark Mills in Scotland when he was 29 at a salary of 1000 pounds a year. Here he started his educational and utopian experiments, and kept them up, while struggling for national factory reforms in England, for a quarter of a century—till he came to the United States. He *succeeded* in his educational and character-building attempts at New Lanark, and got richer all the time. But he wanted to do more. He wanted to change society completely, to give it a new socialist foundation, and that is why he came to the New World.

"Owen was unique among the cotton lords of his day," writes Bestor, "in ascribing his personal success not to his own individual efforts but to the social forces of which he was the beneficiary. There was a normal amount of human vanity in Owen, as his *Autobiography* shows, but it was not the typical conceit of the self-made business-man."[13]

His first pamphlet was *Statement Regarding the New Lanark Esablishment,* Edinburgh, 1812. Then came *A New View of Society; or, Essays on the Principle of the Formation of the Human Character, and the Application of the Principle to Practice,* in 1813-14. After that, his most significant works were: *Observations on the Effect of the Manufacturing System,* 1815; *Report to the Committee for the Relief of the Manufacturing Poor,* 1817; and *On the Employment of Children in Manufactories,* 1818. Then, in 1824, as stated above, he began his New World venture, and gave the important speeches here published.

Owen's *Autobiography* was written in 1857, when he was 85 years old. He died November 17, 1858, in the same town in which he had been born.

---

13. Bestor, *Backwoods Utopias,* p. 64.

Owen himself rejected the charge that he had failed. On his deathbed, he said: "My life was not useless; I gave important truths to the world, and it was only for want of understanding that they were disregarded. I have been ahead of my time."[14]

The special position of Owen as a forerunner of Marxism is indicated in Gustav Mayer's biography of Friedrich Engels. When Engels first came to England as a young man of twenty-two, he attended both the Owenite meetings in the Manchester Hall of Science and the meetings of the first British workers' political movement called the Chartists. "He read the *Northern Star* [Chartist paper] and the *New Moral World* [Robert Owen's paper] with equal eagerness," Mayer writes.[15] Engels contributed an article to Owen's paper, entitled "The Advance of Social Reform on the Continent."

He may not always have agreed fully with either Owenites or Chartists, but he observed, listened, argued and learned. Certainly Engels' *Condition of the Working Class in England in 1844* owed something to Owen's criticism of English manufactories. As to Engels' estimate of the two movements, Mayer says "he was brought to wish that Chartism could be inspired with the spirit of socialism, and socialism with the energy of Chartism, for he felt that the one movement was superior in theory and the other in practice."

Mayer implies that Engels was temperamentally akin to Owen in respect to the latter's social sympathies. Engels' frank admiration for Owen is evident in the statement from *Anti-Dühring*: "Every social movement, every real advance in England on behalf of the workers links itself on to the name of Robert Owen."[16] In his Preface to *The Peasant War in Germany* he classes Owen as "among the most eminent thinkers of all times."[17] Again, in his Preface to the English edition (1892) of *The Condition of the Working Class in England in 1844*, he pays tribute to Owen in saying "since the dying out of Owenism, there has been no socialism in England." He immediately states "there will be socialism again in England," which turned out to be true, but the point here is that Engels regarded Owen as a fellow socialist.[18]

Marx, too, rated Owen highly. In his *Inaugural Address*, 1864, at the founding of the International Workingmen's Association, Marx

---

14. Morton, *Life & Ideas of Robert Owen*, p. 51.
15. Gustav Mayer, *Friedrich Engels*, New York, 1936, p. 43.
16. Engels, *Anti-Dühring*, International Publishers, 1934, p. 290.
17. Marx & Engels, *Selected Works*, Moscow, 1962, Vol. I, p. 652.
18. Marx & Engels, *Selected Works*, Moscow, 1962, Vol. II, p. 417.

took the trouble to point out, first, that "In England, the seeds of the co-operative system were sown by Robert Owen," and second, that Owen had "already in 1816 proclaimed a general limitation of the working day [as] the final preparatory step to the emancipation of the working class."[19] To be sure, these were *reforms*. But when American workers in 1866 made the 8-hour day their basis of struggle, Marx hailed the move. As for cooperatives, it is interesting that early American followers of Marx envisioned the future socialist republic as the "cooperative commonwealth."

While Marx and Engels praised Owen and his fellow utopians, Fourier and St. Simon, for their accomplishments, they also showed where the Utopians were weak. Their writings, said the *Communist Manifesto,* contained an important "critical element," and therefore they were "full of the most valuable materials for the enlightenment of the working class." The Utopians strove in the interests of the workers, but, said the *Manifesto,* they regarded them only as the "most suffering class." They did not regard the workers as a potentially revolutionary class, and were in fact opposed to class struggle and to politics altogether. They appealed, not to the working class, but to the rulers and the rich, in their attempt to change social conditions.

Morton has detailed Owen's weak and strong points. Owen had no faith in the working class, or in class struggle. One of his manifestoes is entitled "An Appeal to the Rich" (1833), and, as we have seen, on his last trip to America, he appealed "To the Capitalists" (1845). In another statement advocating "Revolution by Reason" (1838), Owen said: "This great change . . . must and will be accomplished by the rich and powerful."[20] Furthermore, of course, Owen had no knowledge or understanding of materialist dialectics in philosophy or history or economics or sociology.

But he was a founder of socialism and a forerunner of Marx and Engels. Furthermore, he was a pioneer reformer, being an early champion of labor legislation to reduce hours and improve conditions. He was an initiator of modern educational methods and principles. After his venture in the United States, he had a period of close association with the British trade unions, and in fact, surprisingly enough, played a leading role, rather briefly, in the British labor movement. And he was, says Morton, echoing Marx, "founder, if almost by accident, of the Co-Operative Movement" in England.

19. Marx & Engels, *Selected Works,* Moscow, 1962, Vol. I, pp. 383 & 406.
20. A. L. Morton, *Life & Ideas of Robert Owen,* pp. 125 & 149.

It was this man, this precursor of Marx, who came to the United States in December, 1824, to build socialism through community example. As Leibowitz picturesquely says: "Karl Marx was a seven-year-old school boy in Germany in 1825 when Robert Owen tried his experiment in communism on the banks of the Wabash River at New Harmony, Indiana."

We may say, adapting Morton's dictum,[21] that the world's builders of socialism[22] owe much to Owen; they outgrew him, and had to reject him, but they gratefully remember him.

---

21. Morton, *Life & Ideas of Robert Owen*, p. 53.
22. Professor J. Hampden Jackson of Cambridge University says of the word *socialism* that "the first time it appeared in print was probably November, 1827, when Robert Owen, writing in his *Cooperative Magazine*, said that in the argument whether it is more beneficial that capital should be individual or common there are socialists or communists who held that it should be common." . . . Jackson, J. Hampden, *Marx, Proudhon and European Socialism.* Collier Books, Crowell-Collier Publishing Co., New York, 1962, p. 11. (First published by Macmillan, New York, 1957.)

A

DISCOURSE

on

A NEW SYSTEM OF SOCIETY;

As Delivered in the Hall of Representatives of the United States,

In presence of the President of the United States,
the President Elect, Heads of Departments,
Members of Congress, &c., &c.

on the 25th of February, 1825.

———————

By ROBERT OWEN, of New Lanark.

———————

WASHINGTON:

Printed by Gales & Seaton.

1825.

MR. OWEN'S DISCOURSE

on

A NEW SYSTEM OF SOCIETY

The subject which I shall now endeavor to explain, is, without exception, the most important that can be presented to the human mind. And, if I have been enabled to take a right view of it, then are changes at hand greater than all the changes which have hitherto occurred in the affairs of mankind.

But, if, on the contrary, I have been deceived in my ardent, and earnest, and honest endeavors to discover truth, for the benefit of my fellow-men, then it behooves those distinguished individuals, now before me, and all, indeed, who are interested in the improvement of our species, to take the most effectual means to show wherein I am wrong.

For, believing, as I do, most conscientiously, that the principles which I am about to explain, are founded in fact, are in unison with all nature, and are abundantly competent to relieve society from its errors and evils, I must, while this conviction so remains, adopt every measure that my faculties and experience can suggest, to enable all men to receive the same impressions, and to act upon them.

It is, therefore, no light duty that is about to devolve on those who are to direct the affairs of this extensive Empire. For the time is come when they will have to decide, whether ignorance and poverty, and disunion, and counteraction, and deception, and imbecility, shall continue to inflict their miseries upon its subjects, or whether affluence, and intelligence, and union, and good feeling, and the most open sincerity, in all things, shall change the condition of this population, and give continually increasing prosperity to all the states, and secure happiness to every individual within them. And this is but a part, and a small part, of the responsibility with which they cannot avoid being invested: for it is not merely the ten or twelve millions who are now in these states, who will be injured or essentially benefitted by their decisions; but their neighbors in the Canadas, in the West Indies, and over the whole continent of South America, will be almost immediately affected by the measures that shall be adopted here.

Nor will their responsibility be limited within this new Western world. The influence of their proceedings will speedily operate most powerfully upon the Governments and people of the old world.

If, upon a fair and full examination of the principles which I am to present to you, they shall be found true and most beneficial for practice, those who are appointed to administer the general affairs of the Union, and of the respective states, of which it is composed, will have to decide upon the adoption of measures to enable the people of this continent to enjoy the advantages which those principles and practices can secure to them and to their posterity.

And, through long experience, I am prepared to say, that the advantages to be derived from these principles and practices, will be so superior to any now possessed by any people, that, if the Governments of the old world do not gradually alter their institutions, so as to permit the subjects of their respective states to partake of similar benefits, then will the population of the old world come to the new: for, within its limits, from north to south, there is an abundance of capacity to sustain and support, in high comfort, much more than all the present population of the old world. Therefore, the rulers of these states, in coming to a decision on this subject, will have to decide upon the destinies of the human race, both in this and in future generations.

The knowledge which I possess upon this subject has been derived from reading and reflection, from practice, and from personal communication.

To make myself acquainted with the facts to be collected from the past history of our species, I read, in my early life, at least five hours each day, on an averge of twenty years. This reading was in English, the only language I have acquired, and I know it but imperfectly.

To ascertain whether the principles which the reading of those facts, and the reflections thereon, produced in my mind, were true, and, if true, beneficial for practice, I commenced a series of experiments, which have now continued, without intermission, for nearly thirty-five years.

To make myself quite sure that I could not be deceived in the truth of these principles, in the results of the experiments, or in the advantages to be derived from their universal application to practice, I have employed a considerable portion of each year, of the last twelve, to mix freely with all descriptions of society, and to communicate, in person, confidentially, with the leaders of the various classes, sects, and parties, to be found in my own country, and in the most civilized parts of Europe. I have also, in the same manner, communicated with many strangers, of every rank and condition, who came, as visitors, from different parts of the world, to examine the results of the experiments which I commenced, more than twenty-five years ago, at New Lanark, in Scotland, where they continue in daily successful progress.

Among these strangers, not a few were from this country; for the experiments were made for the benefit of mankind, and they have ever been open to the inspection of all my fellow-creatures, from every quarter of the world.

The result of such reading, reflection, experiments, and personal communication, has been, to leave an irresistible impression on my mind, that society is in error; that the notions on which all its institutions are founded, are not true; that they necessarily generate deception and vice, and that the practices which proceed from them, are destructive of the happiness of human life.

The reflections which I was enabled to make, upon the facts which the history of our race presented to me, led me to conclude that the great object intended to be attained, by the various institutions of every age and country, was, or ought to be, to secure happiness for the greatest number of human beings. That this object could be obtained only, 1st, by a proper training and education, from birth, of the physical and mental powers of *each* individual; 2d, by arrangements to enable *each* individual to procure, in the best manner, at all times, a full supply of those things which are necessary and the most beneficial for human nature; and, 3d, that *all* individuals should be so united and combined in a social system, as to give to each the greatest benefit from society.

These are, *surely*, the great objects of human existence: yet the facts conveyed to us, by history, and the experience of the present, assure us that no arrangements have been formed—that no institutions exist, even to this hour, competent to produce these results. For, is it not a fact, that, at this moment, ignorance, poverty, and disunion, pervade the earth? Are not these evils severely felt in those countries esteemed the most civilized? Do they not now abound in those nations in which the arts and sciences, and general knowledge, and wealth, and political power, have made the most rapid and extensive progress? Then, permit me to ask, Why have these plain and simple, yet most important objects, not been attained? Why has so little real progress been made in the road to substantial happiness? My reading reflection induced me to conclude, that man continued degraded, and poor, and miserable, because he was forced, by the prejudices of past times, to remain ignorant of his own nature, and, in consequence, that he had formed institutions not in unison, but in opposition to it; and thence proceeded the conflict between a supposed duty and his nature.

To aid me in discovering whether this conclusion was true or false, my attention was turned to the examination of facts calculated to assist in forming a right judgment upon the subject. A steady and persevering examination of these facts, confirmed the early impressions made by reading reflection.

The records of history informed me, that human nature had been governed by force and fraud, and that a general conviction prevailed that it could not be otherwise controlled with safety or benefit to itself. Yet, from the most impartial consideration I could give to the past transactions of mankind, I was obliged to conclude that those principles of government proceeded from error regarding the real constitution of human nature.

It seemed to me, that a government founded on justice, kindness, and sincerity, as soon as the world could be induced to admit of sincerity in its transactions, would be one more suited to human nature, and much more likely to improve the condition of any people. To enable me to ascertain the truth or error of these suppositions, at the age of eighteen I commenced a series of experiments upon a limited population.

At that period, circumstances occurred which placed 500 persons— men, women, and children—under my management; and, from that time to this, I have had from 500 to 2,500, the present number, under my immediate direction.

Without any regard to the previous character of these people, I determined to govern them upon principles of strict justice and impartial kindness.

I wished, also, to have adopted a system of open sincerity with all of them; but the irrational state of their minds, of those around them, and of the public at large, at that period, rendered such a proceeding impracticable, and the attempt to introduce a practice so new and strange to the world, would have destroyed my usefulness.

I was, therefore, by the force of circumstances, compelled to reflect much, to speak little, and to practice extensively. And these were my habits during the first twenty years of these experiments.

In all that period, I did not intrude one sentence upon the world: for I deemed it a duty to make myself quite sure of the truth of all the principles upon which I acted, before I recommended them for the adoption of others.

But, during that period, I had a full opportunity of proving the truth and value of the principles which had governed my conduct.

These principles enabled me to proceed, from one step of success to another, until more was accomplished than the world deemed possible to attain in practice. Many would not believe, on any testimony, that such results could be produced, until they came to examine the facts for themselves; and even then it was with difficulty they admitted the evidence of their own senses, many of them exclaiming with astonishment "The beings before me do not appear to belong to the human nature I have been accustomed to see, or with which I have previously associated."

They saw a population that had been indolent, dirty, imbecile, and demoralized, to a lamentable extent, who had become actively industrious, cleanly, temperate, and very generally moral, in all their proceedings. They saw the children of these people trained and educated, from two years of age and upwards, without individual reward or punishment, and they had never seen children who were their equals, in disposition, habits, manners, intelligence, and kind feelings, or who appeared to enjoy an equal degree of active happiness. Yet this population had been so changed by an unknown and uneducated individual, without fortune and friends, and in opposition to almost every conceivable obstacle that the prejudices derived from ages of ignorance, could unite, and while, comparatively, a few only of the circumstances most favorable to well-being and happiness, could be combined for their improvement.

It may now be the wish of many to inquire, Whence this influence? Wherein does its efficacy consist? And by what unheard of means or magic power, are these beneficial, yet strange results, now brought to pass? I reply, by means the most natural, obvious, and simple, and the knowledge of which were obtained from the facts around us; from facts, too, which have been familiar to man in every stage of his existence, and which, as they are derived from the direct evidence of our senses, no intelligent mind will now dispute. For is it not a fact, in accordance with the direct evidence of our senses, that infants at birth, are ignorant of themselves, and of all things around them? Is it not a fact, that they are unconscious how their senses were formed, or any part of their organization was generated or produced? Is it not a fact, that the senses and organization of no two infants have ever been known to be alike, although all possess the same general principles of human nature; and that no two individuals have ever been made the same, although trained and educated under apparently similar external circumstances? Is it not a fact, that all infants are most powerfully influenced by the general and particular external circumstances which exist around them at birth, and through childhood and youth, to manhood?

Is it not a fact, that these circumstances may be so varied, as to give an almost infinite variety of character to any infants, on principles as fixed and certain as those on which any of the sciences are founded; and that, by such varied circumstances, any, or all infants may be trained to become ignorant or intelligent, cruel or humane, selfish or liberal—a Cannibal or Hindoo, a miserable being, or one whose existence shall be a life of happiness? Is it not a fact, that all infants are capable of being formed by the overwhelming influence of circumstances, acting upon their original individual nature, into any of these characters, provided their physical and mental organization be not imperfect: and that, in such case, as nature has been disturbed in her process, that the beings thus injured, physically or mentally, become objects for compassion and for increased care and kindness, in proportion to their malformation? And is it not a clear and evident deduction from these facts, that those who govern society, possess the power, if they knew how to use it, to combine and regulate the circumstances which ought to influence and form the character of every individual of the rising generation? And thus do they possess within themselves, the sure means of creating affluence, intelligence, virtue, and happiness, throughout the whole population.

These are living facts, confirmed by the history of every nation and people, and they are in strict accordance with whatever we know from the evidence of our own senses.

And it was in consequence of acting upon the belief in the truth of these facts, that the characters of those placed under my direction were so much changed for the better, and that their condition has been so materially improved.

With a knowledge of these facts, I could not be angry or displeased with any of those placed under my guidance, on account of any original personal defects; for to me, it was evident they could not have had the slightest influence in producing them. Neither could

I be angry or displeased with them, on account of the injuries which they might have received from being surrounded with unfavorable circumstances, over which they could have had no control, but which circumstances formed their language, dispositions, habits, sentiments, religion, feelings, and conduct. If these were defective and inferior, they necessarily created, in my mind, compassion for their misfortunes, and my thoughts were employed in discovering the circumstances which produced these unfavorable effects, and all my efforts were directed to remove them, and to replace them by others having a beneficial tendency. Having discovered that individuals were always formed by the circumstances, whatever they might be, which were allowed to exist around them, my practice was to *govern* the circumstances, and thus by means imperceptible and unknown to the individuals, I formed them, to the extent I could control the circumstances, into what I wish them to become; and in this manner were the beneficial changes effected in the population under my care. In this process, I could not be disappointed: for I did not expect any evil to disappear, until I had removed the cause or casues which produced it; nor will evil of any kind ever be excluded from Society, until the cause which gives it existence shall be discovered and removed.

Here, then, have we before us the *natural* means by which, on sure grounds, society may be made virtuous, and immediately improved, to an extent that no one can limit; and, by a similar practice, the causes which generate all the inferior motives, and, consequently, actions of man, may be easily withdrawn; and, by the same means, universl charity, benevolence, and kindness, may be made to become the ruling principles in the government of mankind.

With a knowledge of the facts which I have enumerated, relative to the constitution of human nature, the error and childishness of praising and blaming each other, and of devising rewards and punishments, and of applying them, through a gross ignorance of our nature, to particular individuals, must become too obvious to admit of their longer continuance among those who have any real pretensions to rationality.

For what shall we praise or blame each other? Not, surely, for our personal qualifications, which we had no will in forming! Still less for being born within the circle in which Jewish, Christian, Mahommedan, or any other general impressions are, at an early age, forced into our minds! Or do we praise and blame each other because we have come into existence a member of any particular sect, class, or party, in any country, within either of these large circles which now so effectually divide man from his fellow-man, and, in consequence, make him one of the most unjust and irrational of all beings! Or shall we praise or blame each other because we have been born of rich or poor, virtuous or vicious parents; or because the more or less favorable circumstances, existing in the place of our birth and training, made the population around us more or less wise or foolish, strong or weak! Or shall we praise or blame each other for any conceivable combination of our personal or acquired advantages or disadvantages!

In this irrational conduct, behold the real cause of almost all the evils that have ever afflicted humanity, save those extraordinary overwhelming dispensations of Providence, which seldom occur, and soon pass away.

Man, through ignorance, has been, hitherto, the tormentor of man.

He is *here,* in a nation deeming itself possessed of more privileges than all other nations, and which pretensions, in many respects, must be admitted to be true. Yet, even *here,* where the laws are the most mild, and consequently the least unjust and irrational, individuals are punished even to death, for actions which are the natural and necessary effects arising from the injurious circumstances which the government and society, to which they belong, unwisely permit to exist; while other individuals are almost as much injured by being as unjustly rewarded for performing actions for which, as soon as they shall become rational beings, they must be conscious they cannot be entitled to a particle of merit.

It is true that, from obvious causes, the great mass of the people, in all countries, have been so trained by the circumstances around them, that they have been forced, unknown to themselves, to receive notions which are opposed to the great and important truths which I have placed before you, and, in consequence, the most lamentable ignorance of human nature universally prevails, and poverty, and injustice, and vice, and misery, at this hour, everywhere superabound.

Vast numbers of men, and more particularly women, in all countries, have been forced, from generation to generation, to receive, in infancy, as true, various imaginary notions, long prevalent in those countries, and they have been taught that their happiness or misery depended upon their belief or disbelief in the truth of those notions. In various countries, these notions differ materially. In some, they are in direct opposition to others, and, as *all* are trained to think that the

notions taught in their own country are so true that it is impossible
they can be deceived, and that those in opposition to them are so
false that none but the most ignorant and weak will be made to
believe in them, and that such false and wicked notions must produce
vicious conduct: In this manner, every imaginable bad feeling, that
can be implanted in human nature, is generated and fostered. National,
sectarian, and individual antipathies necessarily follow; division and
counteraction, of every description, succeed, and the world is thus
forced to become a chaotic scene of confusion, disorder, and misery.

It is so at this moment, and, strange to say, it has been made to be
so through those original qualities of our nature which, whenever
they shall be rightly directed, and justice shall be done to them, will
produce the fullness of charity, and kindness, and sincerity, from each
to all, until we shall become, in fact and in reality, a new people,
having but one common interest; and then all the benefits of the
world will be freely open to every one, and, in consequence, all will
be gainers, to an extent that no imagination has been yet trained to
be competent to conceive.

The original faculties of our nature, which have been thus abused,
are the natural love of truth, and the desire to benefit our fellow
creatures to the greatest possible extent. These are the genuine
feelings which *now* actuate the conscientiously religious, in all the
countries throughout the world. These are the sole motives which
animated the *real* religious of all the past times, and which gave an
inexpressible pleasure to the dying moments of martyrs of all sects, in
every age and country. Why should these inestimable qualities of the
human mind be longer abused, and forced to become the instruments
of universal discord, confusion, and suffering? Is it wise in those that
govern to allow this wretched error to continue?

Are there not men around me, even now, in the actual possession
of ten fold more power and influence than are requisite to stem this
torrent of error and misdirection of the finest feelings and best
faculties of our nature?

I know there are, and I trust they will now manfully and promptly
step forward, and place themselves in the gap between the present
and the future, and from this Capitol, in their collective capacity, say
to the world, "Now shall the government of force, and fraud, and
disunion cease, and from henceforth truth, and sincerity, and charity,
and kindness, and union, shall take their place, and superstition and
prejudice shall no longer have domination *here*."

This is the mighty deed that the intelligent part of the population of this country, and the enlightened men among all the nations of the earth, will expect at their hand. And can any position be conceived so important, or, at this moment, so highly to be desired, for the accomplishment of the greatest good to this country and to the world, as that to which the new administration of this empire has been just appointed?

Knowing well the favorable circumstances which, in the most extraordinary manner, have been combined, and are in full force to aid its attainment, I conjure them, on account of their own future feelings and reflections, but I conjure them, most particularly, in the name of those innumerable beings throughout the world, who are now afflicted with penury and want, with ignorance, and vice, and superstition, with the inferior motives which have been instilled into their minds from infancy, and the consequent misery which they suffer, that they will not allow this inestimable opportunity to escape. If the leading men of these States, forgetting every little and unworthy party and sectarian distinction, will now cordially unite, they may, with ease, break asunder the bonds of ignorance, superstition, and prejudice, and, by thus acting, they could not fail to dispel error, and to give and secure mental freedom and happiness to the world. To effect this change, the greatest ever yet made in human affairs, no sacrifice on their parts will be necessary. If they possess, as I trust they do, sufficient moral courage to will this deed, and without delay to express that will openly and decisively to the world, then will mental slavery soon cease everywhere, and the victory over ignorance and poverty, and sin, and misery, will be achieved. Here, fortunately for you and for the future destinies of the human race, no regal or legal power sustains ignorance, error, and superstition, and without such support, what chance of success can those have in opposition to the most valuable practical truths, derived immediately from the most obvious facts around us?

The Government and Congress of this new empire have only now, as I have previously stated, to will this change, and it will be at once effected; and, by such act, they will give and secure liberty, affluence, and happiness, to America and to the world.

I have said, give liberty to America; but the natives of this empire have been taught to believe, that they already possess full liberty. I know it is *not* so; and, in proof of this denial, permit me to ask, how many present feel they possess the power to speak their real senti-

ments, freely and openly, on subjects the most important to themselves and to the well being of society? Until this can be done, and
done without any disadvantage whatever to those who do it, liberty
has not been attained, and you have yet to work out for yourselves
this, the most precious and valuable part of liberty. Many must be
now conscious that they are to a great extent under the despotism of
weak minds, who are themselves the slaves of superstition and
prejudice. Until human beings shall, without any inconvenience whatever, speak openly and frankly the genuine impression of their mind
on all subjects, they must be considered to be in a state of mental
bondage, and in that condition all men have ever yet been, and, to a
greater extent, perhaps, than you suspect, you are so even now. By a
hard struggle you have attained political liberty, but you have yet to
acquire real mental liberty, and if you cannot possess yourselves of it,
your political liberty will be precarious and of much less value. The
attainment of political liberty is, however, a necessary step towards
the acquirement of real mental liberty, and as you have obtained the
former, I have come here to assist you to secure the latter. For, without mental liberty, there can be no sincerity; and, without sincerity,
devoid of all deception, there can be no real virtue or happiness
among mankind.

My desire now is, to introduce into these States, and through
them, to the world at large, a new social system, formed in practice
of an entire new combination of circumstances, all of them having a
direct moral, intellectual, and beneficial tendency, fully adequate to
effect the most important improvements throughout society. This
system has been solely derived from the facts relative to our common
nature, which I have previously explained.

In this new social arrangement, a much more perfect system of
liberty and equality will be introduced than has yet anywhere existed,
or been deemed attainable in practice. Within it, there will be no
privileged thoughts or belief; everyone will be at full liberty to express
the genuine impressions, which the circumstances around them have
made on their minds, as well as their own undisguised reflections
thereon, and then no motive will exist for deception or insincerity of
any kind.

Everyone will be instructed in the outline of all the real knowledge
which experience has yet discovered. This will be effected on a plan
in unison with our nature, and by which the equality of the mental
faculties will be rendered more perfect, and by which all will be

elevated much above what any can attain under the existing despotism of mind; and by these arrangements the general intellect of society will be enabled to make greater advances in a year, than it has been hitherto allowed to attain in a century. The innumerable and incalculable evils and absurdities which have arisen from the inequality of wealth, will be effectually overcome and avoided throughout all the future. By arrangements, as simple and desirable as they will be beneficial for everyone, all will possess, at all times, a full supply of the best of everything for human nature, as far as present experience, on these matters, can direct our knowledge.

The degrading and pernicious practice in which we are now trained, of buying cheap and selling dear, will be rendered wholly unnecessary: for, so long as this principle shall govern the transactions of men, nothing really great or noble can be expected from mankind.

The whole trading system is one of deception; one by which each engaged in it is necessarily trained to endeavor to obtain advantages over others, and in which the interest of all is opposed to each, and, in consequence, not one can attain the advantages that, under another and a better system, might be, with far less labor, and without risk, secured in perpetuity to all.

The consequence of this inferior trading system is to give a very injurious surplus of wealth and power to the few, and to inflict poverty and subjection on the many.

In the new system, union and co-operation will supersede individual interest, and the universal counteraction of each other's objects; and, by the change, the powers of one man will obtain for him the advantages of many, and all will become as rich as they will desire. The very imperfect experiments of the Moravians, Shakers, and Harmonites, give sure proof of the gigantic superiority of union over division, for the creation of wealth. But these associations have been hitherto subject to many disadvantages, and their progress and success have been materially counteracted by many obstacles which will not exist under a system, founded on a correct knowledge of the constitution of our nature.

We cannot fail to be alive to the superiority of combined over individual efforts, when applied to destroy. We all know the increased power acquired by a small army, united, and acting as one body, over the same number of men acting singly and alone—and if such advantages can be gained by union to destroy, why should it not be applied to our benefit for civil purposes?

The new combinations proposed will be associations of men possessing real religious and mental liberty, with every means for obtaining great mental acquirements· and these, it is expected, will rapidly increase among all the members.

Under this system, real wealth will be too easily obtained in perpetuity and full security to be much longer valued as it now is by society, for the distinctions which it makes between the poor and rich. For, when the new arrangements shall be regularly organized and completed, a few hours daily of healthy and desirable employment, chiefly applied to direct modern mechanical and other scientific improvements, will be amply sufficient to create a full supply, at all times, of the best of everything for everyone, and then all things will be valued according to their intrinsic worth, will be used beneficially, and nothing will be wasted or abused. I did expect, before this time, to have received from Europe models upon a large scale, of these new combinations, and, without which, it is difficult to comprehend that which is so wholly new in principle and practice to you. I have here drawings of some of them; they are, however, upon too small a scale to be seen by the whole assembly, but I shall have pleasure in opening them after the meeting, for the inspection of any parties who may wish to examine them.

Well knowing the great extent of these advantages, my wish now is to give them, in the shortest time, to the greatest number of my fellow creatures, and that the change from the present erroneous practices should be effected, if possible, without injury to a human being.

With this view, I am prepared to commence the system on my own private responsibility, or with partners having the same principles and feelings with myself; or by joint stock companies, under an act of incorporation from the state governments of Indiana and Illinois, in which the new properties which I have purchased, with a view to these establishments, are situated—or, by a general incorporated company, formed of the leading persons in each state, who could easily form arrangements by which the benefit of the system might be obtained, with the least loss of time, by all the inhabitants within each Government, belonging to the Union. Improbable and impracticable as I well know it must appear to you, and to the mass of the public, I do not hesitate to state confidently from this chair, from which you have been accustomed to hear so many important truths, that the system which I am about to introduce into your states, is fully competent to form them into countries of palaces, gardens, and pleasure grounds, and, in one generaion, to make the inhabitants a race of very superior beings.

When the principles on which this new system is founded, and the practices to which they will necessarily lead, shall be so investigated as to be fully understood, it will be discovered that the present system of society must almost immediately give way before it.

The principles of human nature, on which its morals are founded, will render union and co-operation, to any extent, not only easy, but delightful in practice. The pecuniary effects which will be produced by union and co-operation, will make the division and combination of labor, in the same persons and interest, complete, and, in consequence, all individual competition must prove unavailing, and cause loss of time and capital.

I am, therefore, desirous that the knowledge of this change being about to commence should be speedily known over the Union, that as little capital as possible should be lost by its application to objects which might be rendered of no value by the new measures which may be soon carried into extensive execution in all the states. Many, who have partially considered this subject, and who are converts to the principles, and fully alive to the benefits to be derived from the practice, are, nevertheless, impressed with the belief that the system can advance but slowly, as other great changes have been effected.

This supposition is very natural; it is in unison with the experiences of the past; but their minds have not yet had time to expand to the full extent of this subject, and to discover how different its character is from all former changes. These have been merely an alteration of the mode of acting, while the fundamental principles remained untouched; but, in the present case, there will be an entire change of the fundamental principles on which society has proceeded in all countries, from the earliest period of which we possess knowledge, to the present. Compared with the mighty consequences which must flow from this change, all former revolutions in human affairs scarcely deserve a name.

This is a revolution from a system in which individual reward and punishment has been the universal practice, to one, in which individual reward and punishment will be unpracticed and unknown, except as a grievous error of a past wretched system. On this account, my belief has long been, that, wherever society should be fully prepared to admit of one experiment on the new system, it could not fail to be also prepared to admit the principle from which it has been derived, and to be ready for all the practice which must emanate from the principle; and, in consequence, that the change could not be one of slow progression, but it must take place at once, and make an immediate, and almost instantaneous, revolution in the minds and manners of the society in which it shall be introduced—unless we can imagine that there are human beings who prefer sin and misery to virtue and happiness.

Let the subject be sifted and examined with the most scrutinizing care and caution, and it will prove to be as I have now stated. The truth is, that the great principle on which the new system rests, is directly opposed to that on which old society has been founded; they lead to the same opposition in practice; and there is not the slightest connection between them, nor is it possible they can long exist together. For, whenever these two principles shall be brought into fair and open competition, one or other must speedily prove to be false, and a mere notion of the imagination. The one attributes merit and demerit to belief. The other gives neither merit nor demerit to any belief, because belief has never been under the will or control of man. The one generates in man anger and irritation, because his fellow man differs from him in sentiments, habits, and feelings. The other instructs how men are necessarily made to differ in color, in language, in habits, in sentiments, in religion, in feeling, and in conduct, and thereby implants in everyone the principle of universal charity, benevolence, and kindness, and withdraws all anger from the human constitution. The one separates man from man, individualizing the human race, and thereby creating endless causes of division and opposition of interest and of feeling, and thus generates and fosters all the inferior motives and bad passions and actions which have ever pervaded society. The other forms man at once into a rational being; and, by removing every cause of dislike and jealousy, prepares the most effectual means to unite him with his fellows, and to combine them in one general system of action for their mutual benefit. In short, the one is, in reality, an imaginary notion, which has ever been impressed in infancy on the mind of the human race, in direct opposition to every known fact; a notion derived solely from the ignorance of the darkest ages, and which has so perverted the human faculties as, with slight exceptions, to keep the whole race of men almost continually involved in war and violence, in direct opposition to the real interest of every individual. While the other is a principle derived from experience, in unison with all facts, past and present: a principle which deprecates all war and violence, and punishment of every kind; which harmonises every feeling and faculty of the human mind, rendering it rational and humane, and uniting all in one bond of interest and affection. Therefore, between this principle and imaginary notion, there can be no resemblance whatever; they must adjure each other, the one being the cause of all happiness to man, the other of all misery; and the time is now come when the principle of good is about to predominate and reign triumphant over the principle of evil; and when, in consequence, society may be most easily arranged to exist without ignorance or poverty, or vice, or crime, or misery.

It is to effect this change that I am here this night; that, if possible, a mortal blow shall be now given to the fundamental error which, till now, has governed this wretched world, and inflicted unnumbered cruelties and miseries upon its inhabitants. The time has passed, within the present hour, when this subject can be longer smothered or hidden from the public mind of this country. It must now be open to the most free discussion, and I well know what will be the result.

At this time a match has been applied to a train, that, if I mistake not, will dispel past errors, until old things shall pass away, and all shall become new, and beautiful, and delightful, bringing unnumbered and unlimited blessings to everyone. I trust this subject now appears paramount to every other, and that the necessity for a speedy examination of it, by the highest authorities, is equally evident.

Placed as it now is before the public, a day ought not to be lost in stamping it with its proper terms of truth or falsehood.—The system now advocated can be of no equivocal character; it must be full of benefit or of evil to you all; I therefore beseech you, for your sakes, and for the public benefit, to ascertain its value, that the people may know whether I have brought them a vision to amuse them, or a substantial blessing. To effect this object, may I be permitted to suggest, that competent persons be appointed, under the name of commissioners, or committee, or any other name, to examine the whole subject, a mere outline of which, in this discourse, has been hastily and slightly sketched. That, after such examination, the parties appointed to investigate, make a report, for the satisfaction of the public, whose interests are so deeply involved in the result.

In what has been said, I have endeavored to show, that the subject I have introduced is the most important that can engage the attention of mankind; that the cause of all past and present evil in society is the notion that there can be merit or demerit in any belief whatever; that this error generates all the bad passions, keeps them in perpetual activity, produces nothing but unhappiness to the human race; and that, while it shall be allowed to irrationalise each succeeding generation, sin and misery must have dominion over the world.

I have stated, also, that, by the undeviating constitution of our common nature, each individual has, hitherto, been formed by the circumstances which have been allowed to exist around him from birth to manhood; that these circumstances have been uniformly opposed to our constitution, and consequently of a very injurious character, producing only various degrees of vice and misery. I afterwards explained what appeared to me to be the real constitution of our nature and state; that, when circumstances shall be judiciously combined by those who have acquired an accurate knowledge of it, that each individual of our species, without a single exception, may be trained to become virtuous, intelligent, and happy, to a degree much exceeding what has been experienced under the old system of society in any part of the world. And thus far only time allows me to proceed on the present occasion.

That which requires yet to be explained, to enable the public to form a right judgment of the entire system now advocated, is a detail of the circumstances which, in combination, is to possess sufficient power to produce the extraordinary results which I have promised, and a development of the means by which, without injury to anyone, they can be carried without delay into national and general practice, so as to give, almost immediately, many of the benefits of the change to the whole population of the Union, by relieving them from poverty or the fear of it, and very soon from ignorance, and all the lamentable effects which these two evils necessarily produce.

A

DISCOURSE

on

A NEW SYSTEM OF SOCIETY;

As Delivered in the Hall of Representatives of the United States

In presence of the President of the United States,
the Ex-President, Heads of Departments,
Members of Congress, &c.

on the 7th of March, 1825.

———————

By ROBERT OWEN, of New Lanark.

———————

WASHINGTON:

Printed by Gales & Seaton.

1825.

MR. OWEN'S SECOND DISCOURSE

on

A NEW SYSTEM OF SOCIETY

In my former discourse, from this place, it was stated that the subject which was then brought before you, was the most important that could engage the attention of mankind; that the world was in error, and that all its institutions partook of it; that this error was the notion that man formed his own belief; that merit and demerit belonged to it, and that as long as this error should be forced into the minds of each succeeding generation, at an early age, the human race must continue to be, as heretofore, irrational, and their proceedings to remain as they are, and ever have been—a complicated scene of disorder, counteraction, and confusion.

It was then explained what appeared to me, after much reading, reflection, and experience, to be the constitution of our nature: that it was formed, by the power which originally gave it existence, to be influenced by the circumstances which should surround it, so as to receive any opinion, whether true or false, in accordance with facts or opposed to them, and to become, in consequence, either ignorant or intelligent, miserable or happy; and, as these results were not produced by the will or consent of the individual, no one who experienced them, could rationally become a subject of praise or blame; of reward or punishment.

It was, likewise, stated that I had acted upon these principles for thirty-five years; that I was never disappointed in the results which they produced; that this experiment only confirmed the previous history of human existence, which demonstrated these principles to be unerring, and that whenever they should be judiciously applied in practice, they would always prove successful. The investigation of the subject was, therefore, strongly recommended to the Executive part of the government and to the Members of Congress, that, if the principles should be found true, the people of these States might be enabled, in the shortest time, to partake of the innumerable benefits which the principles are calculated to produce in practice.

The discourse was concluded by stating that many important parts of the subject remained unnoticed, because it was apprehended that the time for the continuance of such a meeting had expired.

It was my intention to have proceeded, the next day, to pay my respects to Mr. Jefferson and Mr. Madison, but many of the audience who were present, on the former occasion, having expressed considerable disappointment that the whole subject was not before them, I consented to remain, to have this opportunity of explaining more of the principles, and the means of carrying them into national and general practice. At the particular desire of some of the distinguished individuals who are present, I will, also, explain some of the details of the measure which were adopted to improve the character and condition of the population at New Lanark, more than twenty-five years ago. Upon this part of the subject, some kind friend has saved me trouble, for, to my surprise, I found, at Mr. Pishey Thompson's, since the last meeting, a copy, just published, of an American edition of some of my early writings, in which, twelve years ago, I gave a narrative of my proceedings, in that establishment, during the first twelve years of the experiment, and, before I conclude, I will, with your permission, read some extracts from this publication. It may be here remarked, that, since that work was written, I have visited personally, or examined the written details of most of the public institutions which have been established in Europe for the improvement of the poor and laboring classes; communicated, personally and confidentially, with the leading men of Europe, and passed through 13 years of the most extensive of my practice, and I have now the satisfaction to state, that these united proceedings confirm, in a remarkable manner, the truth of the principles which, at that early period, I had been led to adopt, and have enabled me to become familiar with the new science of circumstances, by which, without any chance of failure, virtue, intelligence, affluence, and happiness, may be secured to every individual of the rising generations, and by which much may yet be attained for the present generation.

As this subject is of such deep importance to everyone of us, as well as to our children and their descendants, permit me, before I proceed to any practical details, to place shortly before you, for the benefit of the public, a correct statement of the broad principles of the science, and of the general consequences to which they will lead; because, if these are not distinctly impressed on the mind, so as to be fully comprehended and clearly understood, all I may endeavor to explain, relative to measures of detail, will be of little or no practical value.

Then it should be ever remembered, that the first principle of the science is derived from the knowledge of the facts, *that external circumstances may be so formed as to have an overwhelming and irrestible influence over every infant that comes into existence, either for good or evil; to compel him to receive any particular sentiments or habits, to surround him, through life, with the most agreeable or disagreeable objects, and thus, at pleasure, make any portion, or the whole of the human race, poor, ignorant, vicious, and wretched; or affluent, intelligent, virtuous, and happy.*

And thus, also, form man to understand and to practice pure and genuine religion, which never did nor ever will consist in unmeaning phrases, forms, and ceremonies; but in the daily, undeviating practice, in thought, word, and action, of charity, benevolence, and kindness, to every human being with whom we come into communication, or have any transactions, near or remote. Now this, and this alone, is true religion, and true, because it will lead to the greatest happiness that man can enjoy, and because it is consistent and in unison with all the facts of which we have been permitted to acquire any knowledge relative to *our* nature and to *all* nature. And, except in this consistency, there is no other criterion of truth.

But this is not the religion of any particular person, age, or country; it is the *universal religion* of human nature. It is *true*—it therefore requires no name for its support, for truth will always support itself, without any facticious aid; and a name can be of no other use than to sanction fraud or error. This universal religion, as I trust it will speedily become, is, therefore, justly called *rational religion*—its base is simple truth, and it defies what man, through error, can do against it. For this rational religion, now, for the first time, declared amidst this enlightened assembly, composed of the most distinguished men of this country, within its metropolis, and within its capitol, I, as a citizen of the world, claim for it the full and complete protection which the American Constitution freely offers to mental and religious liberty. I claim this protection, however, not with the slightest feeling of hostility to a single individual of the human race; my intention is to do them good—to relieve them from the error and evil by which they are now on all sides beset; and my sole object in thus claiming protection for this new religion, is to introduce into practice, and permanently secure, peace and good will among all mankind, by destroying the selfish and establishing the social system.

If these principles proceed from error, they will come to naught;

but if they are consistent with all facts, and, therefore, true, who shall prevail against them?

Having then discovered, as I believe I have, the science of the influence of circumstances, and a rational, and, therefore, a pure and genuine religion, the next important consideration is, to ascertain in what manner the new science and the new religion can be applied, to produce the promised practical results. I have been frequently urged to apply these principles to the present state of society, and not attempt to disturb it, but endeavor to make them unite harmoniously together. To this request I would most willingly accede, if it was practicable. The inventor of the Steam Engine might as well have been required to unite his new machinery with the inefficient and clumsy horse engine, which, at that time, was commonly used to obtain mechanical force: or the inventor of the Spinning Machinery, to unite it with the woollen and flax single wheels; or the person who introduced the gas lights, to combine it with the common candle. These things are impracticable, and everyone knows that, to attempt to effect any of them, would be a loss of time and labor; in like manner, were I to endeavor to unite the system which I advocate, with the present notions and practices of society, my time and labor would be uselessly employed.

The fact is, and I am most anxious that all parties should fully understand me, the system which I propose now for the formation and government of society, is founded on principles, not only altogether different, but directly opposed to the system of society which has hitherto been taught and practised at all times, in all nations. And, until the public mind can be elevated to this point, I shall not be understood; my attempt at explanation must fail to be comprehended, and an inexplicable confusion of ideas will alone remain. The error must be mine; I have not yet been sufficiently explicit; but, upon this occasion, I must endeavor to put the contrast between the two systems, in such a point of view as not to be misunderstood. The old system of the world, by which I mean all the past and the present proceedings of mankind, presupposes that human nature is originally corrupt—that man forms his own belief and his own character—that, if these shall be formed in a particular manner, the individual will deserve an artificial reward, both here and hereafter; but if this belief and this character shall not be so formed, the individual will deserve an artificial punishment both here and hereafter. The theory of the old system is, therefore, founded on notions directly opposed to our nature, and its practice is individual rewards and punishments.

The new system presupposes that human nature is now what it ever has been, and will be, and what the power which produced it formed it to be originally; that man does not create his own belief or his own character, physical or mental; that his belief and character are uniformly created for him, and that he cannot possess merit or demerit for the formation of either; that he is a compound being, formed by the impressions made by external circumstances, upon his individual nature, and, as he had no will, or knowledge, or power, in deciding upon the creation of either, he cannot become a rational object for individual reward or punishment; that man is a being formed to be irresistibly controlled by external circumstances, and to be compelled to act according to the knowledge which those circum stances produce in him; that a knowledge of this fact will compel him to make himself acquainted with the nature of circumstances, so as to understand the effects which they will produce on human nature, and, through that knowledge, compel him to govern all circumstances, within his control, for the benefit of his own and succeeding genera- tions.

The old system has been influenced in all ages, by some imaginary notions or other, under the name of religion, but which notions have been, in all countries, uniformly opposed to facts, and, in consequence, all minds have been thereby rendered more or less irrational. The new system, as I have previously stated, adopts a religion derived from the facts which demonstrate what human nature really is, and which facts give to man all the knowledge he possesses respecting himself; it is, therefore, called rational religion, or a religion of demonstrable truth, of intelligence, and of universal charity and benevolence, and derived from the evidence of our senses.

The old system keeps its votaries in ignorance, makes them mere localized beings, and the perpetual slaves of a combination of the most inferior and worst circumstances, and, in consequence, society is a chaos of superstition, passion, prejudice, poverty in many, and ignorance of their real interest in all; while the new system makes man familiar with his true interests, and, in consequence, gives him the knowledge and power to combine and govern circumstances in such a manner as to secure it, and unerringly to produce happiness to himself and others.

And this is the practical point at which I wished to arrive to produce benefit from this discourse. In my former address, I stated that, to produce the greatest happiness for the greatest number, three things were necessary:

1st. A proper training and education, from birth, of the physical and mental powers of each child.

2d. Arrangements to enable each individual to procure, in the best manner, at all times, a full supply of those things which are necessary and the most beneficial for human nature; and

3d. That all individuals should be so combined in a social system as to give to each the greatest benefits from society.

Now, practical arrangements to produce these results have never yet been formed, or anything approaching to them. They cannot be found in any single and detached dwelling, or in any village, town, or city, in any part of the world. I am, therefore, justified in saying, that, like old machines, when a new one of very superior powers has been invented to supersede them, separate dwelling houses, villages, towns, and cities, must give place to other combinations.

Now, if circumstances possess an overwhelming and irresistible influence over the whole human race, so as to make every individual either happy or miserable, is it not of the last importance to all of us, to become learned in that science, an accurate knowledge of which will enable the present generation to remove misery from the succeeding one, and secure happiness to their posterity?

What other subject can be brought into comparison with this? Or rather, when compared with it, do not all other subjects either lose their value or become extremely insignificant?

If I am right, the first and most important inquiry for human beings ought to be, to ascertain *what* circumstances produce *evil,* and what *good,* and *how* circumstances can be arranged to *produce* the *latter,* and *exclude* the *former.* To become learned in these matters of the deepest interest to my fellow men, has been the study and practice of my life, and as the result of such study and practice, I submit for your most serious consideration the new combination of circumstances which are now before you. They have been very hastily put together by Mr. Hutton, of this City, since our last meeting, and cannot be expected to give more than a very imperfect sketch of the outline of the plan, as it will appear in actual practice.

I am now prepared to say, with a confidence that fears no refutation, and which nothing, except being fully master of the whole subject, could so impress on my mind, that all existing external human or artificial circumstances must speedily give place to these. And, as the essential interests of each one, whatever may be his present rank, station, or condition, in the world, will be promoted, to an incalculable extent, by the change, I trust that one and all, who are present, and the whole American population, will now begin to study the subject, and, when masters of it, assist each other with all their power to remove, speedily, the present wretched and irrational circumstances, and to replace them by others which must, of necessity, make them intelligent and happy.

A model of the combinations to produce those beneficial results is now before you, and such buildings, with a variation of architecture, according to local circumstances, and the views of the parties who form them, placed within 1,000 or 2,000 acres of land, cultivated like a garden, and laid out as pleasure grounds, will be, I presume, the future habitation of the human race.

I express myself thus decisively, because, by a combination of singular circumstances, by long study and experience, I have been permitted to acquire some knowledge on this subject unknown to others.

The model before you contains an arrangement, purposely formed, to enable each individual to possess, in perpetuity, and enjoy, through life, without anxiety, the three objects which have been enumerated, and it may be justly considered to be a new machine for performing, in a superior manner, all the purposes of human life.

Before any rational arrangements could be made for an improved society, it became necessary to ascertain what numbers of persons could be associated together, to give to each the greatest advantages with the fewest inconveniences; that is, to combine the most desirable benefits which the country and cities afford; adding to these the best arrangements for education, from infancy to manhood, the best and most economical arrangements for producing from agriculture and manufactures, for consuming their productions; then uniting the whole to form a social system in which there should be but one interest, and in which each individual should go on continually from one step of improvement to another, acquiring thereby the highest and purest enjoyments of which our nature is susceptible.

Such are the principles on which the arrangements before you have been formed.

The model represents a square of buildings, each side of which is 1,000 feet in length, and each side contains every domestic arrangement that can be required for 5,000 persons. The square is also intended to contain a complete school, academy, and university, in which a superior education will be given from infancy to maturity, and it will comprise the first combination of circumstances which has yet been formed to do anything like justice to the physical and mental powers of any human being. The four buildings within the square, one of which projects from the centre of each of the sides, contain the culinary arrangements, the dining apartments, stores, washing, drying, brewing, and every other domestic accomodation, arranged in a superior manner, by men of great science and practical experience. The schools, lecture rooms, laboratories, chapels, ball and concert rooms, conversation rooms, committee and other public rooms, are in the centres and angles of the building. The private dwellings of the inhabitants are between the centres and angles, and occupy the first and second story. The third story contains the dormitories for the unmarried persons, and children above two years of age. There is a communication under cover, from each dwelling to every other, and to all the public rooms, throughout the whole extent of the square. Each apartment will be heated, cooled, ventilated, supplied with gas lights, and hot or cold water, at the will of the occupants, by merely turning a cock or moving a slide. All the apartments may be cooled in warm weather much below, and warmed in cold weather much above, the temperature of the atmosphere, and under these scientific domestic arrangements, one person, chiefly employed in an interesting direction of mechanical and chemical operations, will perform as much as twenty, under the separate individual system, can accomplish in the same time. By these new arrangements, two essential objects will be secured; the operative or producer will be better trained and educated than the working or any class has been heretofore, and they will be supported at a less expense than must be incurred under any individual system, which can afford but one-half of the advantages that these new arrangements will secure to everyone, even from the commencement. Under these circumstances, therefore, manual and mental power would be produced of a superior quality, and maintained at a less expenditure than under the separate or individual system; consequently, all other circumstances being supposed to be the same, whatever these united labors produce, whether from agriculture or manufactures, will be better and cheaper than similar productions can be brought to market by any individual, seeing that the cost of all productions consists in the value of the labor they contain. Upon this principle, now universally admitted, the present buildings in the country, in villages, towns, and cities, will as rapidly disappear as the new combinations before you can be introduced into practice.

This combination, however, will not only create a superior quality of labor, and support it, in more comfort, at a much less expense than any individual system, but it will place the parties under the most favorable circumstances for gardening, agricultural, and manufacturing operations, which will be so united as to enable each to assist the others, at the different seasons of the year, in such a manner as to secure seed and harvest operations with one-fourth of the favorable weather required in farms and gardens under the present system.

In short, the advantages of this new combination, for health, for forming a superior character, for producing, for consuming, for securing, free from all pecuniary anxieties, the chief benefits, without the disadvantages, of a country, city, and college life, and for enjoying the best society in the most convenient manner, will be discovered to offer such overwhelming temptations to human nature to change from the present system that I conclude it will be impracticable to provide these new abodes of rational improvement and enjoyment, as speedily as society will desire to possess them.

When these buildings, gardens, and pleasure grounds, shall be formed, the next important inquiry is, how are they to be governed?

To explain this part of the subject, I will, with your permission, now read some rules and regulations* which were drawn up, two or three years ago, for an independent society, to be formed of the operative classes, upon the supposition that they borrowed all the capital.

Such are the rules and regulations which are proposed and recommended for an association of the operative classes, on these new principles of union and co-operation, and I have no doubt, but the plain good sense and practical knowledge of many among those classes, will be found, with very little assistance, sufficient to understand the principles, and to carry them into practice upon borrowed capital, what security could be offered superior to that which they could give? Namely, land well chosen for their purpose, and bought at its present value; buildings erected, to be much more convenient, and, therefore, in the same proportion, more valuable than any existing buildings; the land annually improving, by an extensive and

---

*See at the end.

improved cultivation, and manufactures established under the latest improvements; these, added to the security of an association of from 1000 to 2000 industrious and temperate persons, each aiding and none opposing each other, would present such an aggregate of substantial security, continually improving, as is not to be found, perhaps, under any other circumstances. I hope the government of all the states composing the Union, will investigate the whole of this subject, in such a manner as to enable the citizens of each state to become fully satisfied that the principles on which it rests, are so true, that error cannot be found in them, and the practice so beneficial, that it will be evidently the interest of one and all to adopt it with the least delay, that not one day more of unnecessary anxiety and suffering should be experienced by the inhabitants of this country.

But, whatever others may do, my purpose is fixed—I mean to carry these measures of amelioration to the full extent of my means and influence, into immediate execution.

With this view, I have purchased from the Harmonite Society, the settlement and property of Harmony, in the state of Indiana and Illinois. The settlement, or town of Harmony, is upon the Wabash, in Indiana; it is composed of log, weather boarded, and brick dwelling houses; of infant manufactures, of wool, cotton, leather, hats, pottery, bricks, machinery, grain, distilleries, breweries, &c. &c., with granaries, and two large Churches, and other public buildings, laid out in regular squares like all the modern American towns. It does not, however, form such a combination as the model before you represents, and, therefore, it will serve only a temporary, but yet a useful temporary purpose, for the objects which I have in view. It will enable me to form immediately a preliminary society in which to receive a new population, and to collect, prepare, and arrange the materials for erecting several such combinations, as the model represents, and of forming several independent, yet united associations, having common property, and one common interest. These new establishments will be erected upon the high lands of Harmony, from two to four miles from the river, and its Island, of which the occupants will have a beautiful and interesting view, there being several thousand acres of well cultivated land, on a rich second bottom, lying between the highlands and the river. And here it is, in the heart of the United States, and almost the centre of its unequalled internal navigation, that that power which directs and governs the universe and every action of man, has arranged circumstances which were far beyond my control, to permit me to commence a new empire of peace and good will to man, founded on other principles, and leading to other practices than those of the past or present, and which principles, in due season, and in the allotted time, will lead to that state of virtue, intelligence, enjoyment, and happiness, in practice, which has been foretold by the sages of past times, would, as some distant period, become the lot of the human race! Do not the dissatisfaction of all minds, in all countries, with the existing circumstances; the evident advance of just, kind, and benevolent feelings, and the universal expectation of some great change in human affairs, indicate and foretell this change? Do they not give assurance that the time is at hand, when evil shall give place to good—division to union—war to peace—anger to kindness—superstition to charity, and pure practical religion—prejudice to intelligence—and pain and misery to enjoyment and happiness? Assuredly they do, and it will be wise and prudent in us to be prepared for the event.

I have, however, no wish to lead the way; I am most desirous that Governments should become masters of the subject, adopt the principles, encourage the practice, and thereby retain the direction of the public mind for its own benefit, and the benefit of the people. But, as I have not the control of circumstances to ensure success in this public course, I must, as I have stated, shew what private exertions, guided by these new principles, can accomplish at Harmony, and these new proceedings will commence there early in April. It was currently reported, when I arrived in this country, that Harmony was unhealthy, and, in consequence, I had nearly given up the intention which I entertained, of purchasing it, but having crossed the Atlantic with the intention of examining for myself, and knowing from personal experience, how little truth is generally to be found in reports connected with anything new in society, I proceeded to the place and examined the facts in person. I then discovered that for the first three years after the Harmonites made the settlement, the colony was very unhealthy, and this naturally gave rise to the reports. From that period, however, the settlement has become every year more healthy, and for several years past, it has been remarkably so, until the year before last, out of 800, five died, and last year, from the same number, two only died. The change has no doubt arisen from the land being well drained and cultivated, and the woods being extensively cleared. These operations will be now soon more extended, and I conclude that the future inhabitants of Harmony, under their rational mode of life, will be as healthy as the same number of persons in any part of the world.

I have drawn out a prospectus of a preliminary society to be established at Harmony, until arrangements can be formed to enable the parties who meet there to commence the new system according to its genuine principles and practices.

I have been asked, what would be the effect upon the neighborhood and surrounding country, where one or more of these societies of union, co-operation, and common property, should be established?

My conviction is, that, from necessity and inclination, the individual or old system of society, would break up, and soon terminate; from necessity, because the new societies would undersell all individual producers, both of agricultural productions, and manufactured commodities. And from inclination, because it is scarcely to be supposed that anyone would continue to live under the miserable, anxious, individual system of opposition and counteraction, when they could with ease form themselves into, or become members of, one of these associations of union, intelligence, and kind feeling.

If, then, it has been further asked of me, these societies spread by their successful commercial operations, and the increased comforts and advantages which they offer to the whole population, what effects will they have upon the Government and the general prosperity of an extensive empire?

I again reply, that, a country, however extensive, divided into these arrangements of improved social buildings, gardens, and pleasure grounds, and these occupied and cultivated by persons possessing superior dispositions, habits, and intelligence, will be governed with much more ease than it can be with the same number of inhabitants, scattered irregularly over the country, living in common villages, towns, or cities, under the individual system. And that the expense of the government would be diminished as much as the trouble and anxiety. It is not unlikely that these would be diminished to one-tenth of their present amount. The effects which would be produced on the general prosperity of the country, would be equally important and beneficial.

It may, perhaps, with confidence be stated, that any country will be prosperous in proportion to the number, and physical and mental superiority of its inhabitants. Now, the system of union, common property, and co-operation proposed, will, from the same soil, support, in high comfort, double numbers, at the least, and hence its commercial superiority over the individual arrangements of society. And by this improved system, especial care is taken that each child, without a single exception, shall, by a superior training and education, under the most favorable circumstances, have full justice done to all his physical and mental faculties, and by these means a whole population will be formed, each full of bodily and mental health and vigor. There will be, therefore, upon the same soil, a double population, each of whom, through a wise arrangement of circumstances, will be a superior being, when compared with the mere localized man, which the individual system has hitherto formed, and, while it is retained, must everywhere produce.

For defence against the attack of such irrational nations as may surround a country so peopled, the boys, while at school, for their exercise, might be taught military and naval tactics in the best manner, and they would soon become, and present such a force as to be impenetrable from without, and they would have minds too rational, intelligent, and benevolent, ever to be led into offensive warfare.

These communities are in complete union with the principles on which the constitution of this country is founded. The constitution is essentially a government of the union of independent states, acting together for their mutual benefit. The new communities would stand in the same relation to their respective State Governments, that the States do now to the General Government, and, in consequence, the arduous duties of both will be, most probably, materially diminished.

I may further add, that the system is one of genuine liberty and equality, being, in fact, the only system which contains the principles that can produce sufficient individual and general practical virtue to admit of the full enjoyment of the inestimable blessings of full liberty and equality. Ignorance and vice require restraints, but virtue and intelligence need them not.

Such, then, being the overwhelming advantages of the united social over the individual selfish system, permit me to ask, what can support the latter much longer, against the former? And why should not the united social system be now adopted by every intelligent mind?

Allow me to add, that, in supporting the new system in opposition to the old, to do justice to the former, I am frequently under the necessity of using strong expressions, and I fear I must occasionally hurt the feelings of persons who have been trained to have a high respect, and even veneration, for what I am obliged to think the errors of the old system. If there be any such present, I request their forgiveness, and I assure them, that, except in the cause of a high and important duty, paramount to every other consideration, it is quite contrary to all my feelings and principles to say anything to offend those from whom I am obliged to differ in opinion, and if I have so offended anyone on the present or former occasion, I beg it may be attributed to the real cause, the love of truth, and an ardent desire to relieve my fellowmen from the sufferings which they experience.

(Here Mr. O. read, from a work, of which he had met with a copy at Mr. Thompson's Book Store in this city, an account of the Experiment at New Lanark, its Schools, &c.)

This was the origin of the new infant schools which are now spreading rapidly over the British Isles. The singular good effects which were seen to arise from these, induced Mr. Brougham, Mr. John Smith, M. P., the Marquis of Landsdown, and other gentlemen, to form one at their own expense in the Metropolis, to exhibit to the public the incredible results which they could be made to produce.

For this purpose, they were supplied with a master from New Lanark, about four years ago, and he remains at the head of that establishment.

From this infant school many similar ones have been formed, and are now in active operation, both in London and many of the provincial towns, and also in some villages. Experience induces me to say, that this is the most important step, imperfect as it is, that has yet been made in a rational system of instruction. The good effects of them are incalculable, and the expense is very inconsiderable.

A NEW SOCIETY
IS ABOUT TO BE COMMENCED AT HARMONY, IN INDIANA.

The direct object of this association is to give and secure happiness to all its members.

This object will be obtained by the adoption of a system of union and co-operation, founded on a spirit of universal charity, derived from a correct knowledge of the constitution of human nature.

The knowledge thus derived, will be found abundantly sufficient to reconcile all religious and other differences.

But, to insure success in practice, a preliminary society will be organized, and directed by those who understand the principles of this system, and who have already proved them by a partial yet extensive practice.

Into this preliminary society respectable families and individuals, with capital, and industrious and well disposed families and individuals, without capital, will be received.

Those who possess capital, and who do not wish to be employed, may partake of the benefits of this society on paying a sum annually, sufficient to recompense the society for their expenditure.

Those without capital, will be employed, according to their abilities and inclinations, in building, in agriculture, in gardening, in manufactures, in mechanical trades, in giving instruction in elementary or scientific knowledge, or in some one useful occupation, beneficial to the society.

In return for which, they will be provided with the best lodging, food, and clothing, that the circumstances of the establishment will afford: they will experience every attention during sickness and in old age. All the children will be brought up together, as members of the same family, and will receive a good and superior education.

At the end of every year, a certain amount, in value, will be placed to the credit of each family, and each individual, not being a member of a family, in proportion to their expenditure, and to the services rendered by them to the society.

Anyone may leave the society at any time, and take with them, in the productions of the establishment, as much in value, as shall be placed to their credit at the annual balance immediately preceding the time when they cease to become members of the society.

During the continuance of the preliminary society, any family, or individual, whose conduct may be injurious to the well being and happiness of the association, and obstruct its progress, will be removed; but it is expected that the spirit of charity, justice, forbearance, and kindness, which will direct the whole proceedings of the society, and which will be soon diffused through all its members, will speedily render the dismissal of anyone unnecessary.

As soon as circumstances will permit, it is intended that a society shall be formed, consistent in all respects with the constitution of human nature, the general principles and practices of which are explained in the pre-fixed paper, entitled "An outline of a new system of society, recommended for immediate and general practice, by Robert Owen, of New Lanark:" and in this society all will be equal in rights and property, and the only distinction will be that of age and experience.

Members of the preliminary society, who shall acquire such a knowledge of the principles of the new system, as to enable and induce them to apply them to practice, may become members of this more perfect association, in which, it is anticipated, from experiments already tried, during thirty-five years, that almost, if not all the causes which have hitherto produced evil in the world, will be gradually removed.

GENERAL RULES AND REGULATIONS,

Proposed by Mr. OWEN, *for an Independent Community,*
subject to such alterations as circumstances may indicate.

IT IS PROPOSED,—

I. That the community shall consist of persons who have agreed to co-operate, with their labor and skill, in measures for producing, distributing, and enjoying, in the most advantageous manner, a full supply of the necessaries and comforts of life; and for securing for their children the best physical and intellectual education.

II. That, at the commencement, the number of persons shall not much exceed five hundred, including their families.

III. That, as it is of great importance that the Community should produce within itself a full supply of the first necessaries of life, there shall be attached to the establishment a sufficient extent of LAND to render it essentially *agricultural*.

IV. That a Village to be situated as near the centre of the Land as local circumstances may permit, be built according to the plan and elevations given in the engravings.

In this village, the dwelling houses, dormitories, &c. form the sides of a large square; in the centre of which are placed the requisite public buildings, surrounded by public walks and exercise grounds. This form has been adopted as giving superior accommodation to the dwelling houses, and admitting the application at the least expense of scientific improvements in all the departments of domestic economy.

V. That the manufactories, work-shops, granaries, stores, washing and drying houses, be placed at the most convenient distance beyond the gardens which surround the village; and that the farm offices be situated according to the localities of the land.

VI. That, whenever the capital advanced by its own members shall have been repaid, and the education of all be sufficiently advanced, the management of the establishment shall be confined to a committee, composed of all the members between certain ages; as, for example, between forty and fifty. But that, until *such period,* the committee shall consist of twelve persons, to be elected at an Annual General Meeting; eight to be chosen from among those members who have advanced capital to the amount of 100L or upwards, and four from the other members. The committee to be empowered to elect the Treasurers and Secretaries.

VII. That the Treasurers be empowered to receive all moneys due to the community, and pay its disbursements on orders signed by the Secretary. That they balance and report their accounts every week to the committee, who shall appoint two of their number to examine and pass them under their signatures.

VIII. That the Secretary be directed to keep a regular detailed daily statement of all the accounts and transactions of the community, and that such statement be presented weekly to the committee. and submitted to the examination of two of their number, who shall pass it under their signatures, with such observations as may occur to them.

IX. That the books of accounts and transactions of the society be open to the inspection of all its members.

X. That the business of the community be divided into the following departments:

1. Agriculture and gardening.
2. Manufactures and trades.
3. Commercial transactions.
4. Domestic economy: comprehending the arrangements for heating, ventilating, lighting, cleaning, and keeping in repair dwellinghouses and public buildings of the village; the arrangements connected with the public kitchens and dining halls; those for the furnishing of clothes, linen, and furniture, and for washing and drying; and the management of the dormitories.
5. Health, or the medical superintendence of the sick, including arrangements to prevent contagion or sickness.
6. Police, including the lighting and cleansing the square; the repairing of the roads and walks; guarding against fire, and the protection of the property of the community from external depredation.
7. Education, or the formation of character from infancy: to this department will also belong the devising the best means of recreation.

XI. That, for the general superintendence of these departments, the committee appoint sub-committees from their own number, or from the other members of society; each of the sub-committees shall lay a weekly report before the committee, to be examined and passed, with such observations as may be deemed necessary.

XII. That, should there not be, at first, a sufficient number of persons in the community, fully competent to the management of the different branches of industry, which it may be desirable to establish, the committee be empowered to engage the assistance of skilful practical men from general society.

XIII. That, in regulating the employments of the members according to their age, abilities, previous acquirements, and situation in life, the committe pay every regard to the inclinations of each, consistent with the general good; and that the employment be so ordered as to permit every individual, who may be so disposed, to occupy part of his time in agriculture.

Great facilities will be afforded to agriculture by the power which the community will always possess of calling out an extra number of hands, at those times and seasons when it is of the utmost importance to have additional aid.

XIV. That, as under the proposed arrangements, every invention for the abridgment of human labor will bring an increase of benefit to all, it be a primary object with the committee to introduce, to the utmost practical extent, all those modern scientific improvements, which, if rightly applied, are calculated to render manual labor only a healthy and agreeable exercise.

XV. That the first object of the community be to produce a full supply of the necessaries and comforts of life for domestic consumption; and, as far as localities will permit, directly from their own land and labor.

XVI. That, in regard to domestic consumption, each member of the community shall be fully supplied with the necessaries and comforts of life.

XVII. That, within the community, all the members be in equal rights and privileges, according to their respective ages.

XVIII. That, to avoid the evils arising from a system of credit, the commercial transactions of the community be conducted for ready money or barter, only; that these transactions, on the part of the community, be always performed in good faith, and without the slightest attempt to deceive buyer or seller; and that, when any individuals with whom they deal, show a disposition to impose upon the community, all dealings with such individuals shall from that time cease.

XIX. That the surplus proceeds of the united exertions of the community, which remain after discharging rent, interest, taxes, and other expenses, be regularly applied to liquidation of the capital borrowed upon the establishment; and, when this debt is cancelled, it is proposed that the future surplus be invested to form a fund for the establishment of a second community, should the increased population of the first require it.

XX. That, in the domestic department, the following arrangements and regulations be adopted:

1. The heating, ventilating, and lighting of the dwelling houses and public buildings shall be effected according to the most approved methods.
2. An ample supply of water shall be provided, and distributed to each building, for domestic purposes and as a security against fire.
3. Provisions of the best quality, only, shall be cooked in the public kitchen, and it shall be a special object to those persons who have the direction of this department, to ascertain and put in practice the best and most economical means of preparing nutritious and agreeable food. Any parties being ill, or desirous of having their meals alone, may have them sent to their private apartments.
4. The furniture of dwelling houses, dormitories, and public buildings, (as far as the same be provided out of the public funds,) shall be devised in reference to intrinsic use and comfort. A similar regulation will apply to the clothing of the community. Among the children, very essential improvements may be introduced, which will not only save much useless expense, but be the means of increasing in a very high degree, the strength of the constitution.
5. The dormitories designed for the children above two years of age, and those for the youth of the community, until the period of marriage, shall be divided into compartments, and furnished with accommodations suited to the different ages.

XXI. That the employments of the female part of the community consist, in preparing food and clothing; in the care of the dwelling-houses, dormitories, and public buildings; in the management of the washing and drying-houses; in the education (in part) of the children, and other occupations suited to the female character. By the proposed domestic arrangements, *one* female will, with great ease and comfort, perform as much as *twenty* menial servants can do at present; and instead of the wife of a working man, with a family, being a drudge and a slave, she will be engaged only in healthy and cleanly employments, acquire better manners, and have sufficient leisure for mental improvement and rational enjoyment.

XXII. That it be a general rule, that every part of the establishment be kept in the highest state of order and neatness, and that the utmost personal cleanliness be observed.

XXIII. That the following objects and regulations, connected with the department of health, be attended to and adopted:

1. That, on the first appearance of indisposition in any of the members, immediate attention be given to it, and every possible care be taken of the patient till complete recovery; the prevention of serious complaints being always far more easy than to effect a cure after the disease has fixed itself in the constitution.

2. The complaint of indisposition by any individual, shall place him or her on the invalid list, on which the patient will remain until the medical attendant pronounce complete recovery.

3. The arrangements of the apartments for the sick shall be such as to afford every possible comfort to patients, and provide much more effectual means of recovery than their private dwellings could admit of.

4. Removal to the apartments for the sick, shall be at the option of the individual.

5. As the health of the community may be materially improved or injured by the interior plan of the dwelling-houses, by their situation with respect to other buildings, by dress, food, employment, the temper and general state of the mind, and by various other circumstances—the attention of the sub-committee of this department, shall be constantly directed to this important consideration.

XXIV. That, as the right education of the rising generation is, under Divine Providence, the base upon which the future prosperity and happiness of the community must be founded, the committee shall regard this as the most important of all the departments committed to their direction, and employ in its superintendence those individuals whose talents, attainments, and dispositions, render them best qualified for such a charge.

The children of the community shall be educated together, and as one family, in the schools and exercise grounds provided for them in the centre of the square; where they will at all times be under the eye and inspection of their parents.

By properly conducting their education, it will be easy to give each child good tempers and habits; with as sound a constitution as air, exercise and, temperance, can bestow:

A facility in reading, writing, and accounts;

The elements of the most useful sciences, including geography and natural history;

A practical knowledge of agriculture, and domestic economy, with a knowledge of some ONE useful manufacture, trade, or occupation, so that this employment may be varied, for the improvement of his mental and physical powers;

And, lastly, a knowledge of himself and of human nature, to form him into a rational being, and render him charitable, kind, and benevolent, to all his fellow-creatures.

XXV. That, when the youth of the community shall have attained their sixteenth year, they be permitted either to become members, or to go out into general society, with every advantage which the community can afford them.

XXVI. That intelligent and experienced matrons be appointed to instruct the young mothers in the best mode of treating and training children from birth until they are two years old (the age at which it is proposed to send them to the schools and dormitories) that their constitutions, habits, and dispositions, may not be injured during that period.

XXVII. That, in winter and unfavorable weather, a sufficient variety of amusements and recreations, proper for the members of such a community, be prepared within doors, to afford beneficial relaxation from employment and study.

XXVIII. That, as liberty of conscience, religious and mental liberty, will be possessed by every member of the Community, arrangements be made to accommodate all denominations with convenient places of worship, and that each individual be strongly recommended to exhibit in his whole conduct the utmost forbearance, kindness, and charity towards all who differ from him.

XXIX. That in advanced age, and in case of disability from accident, natural infirmity, or any other cause, the individual shall be supported by the community, and receive every comfort which kindness can administer.

XXX. That on the death of parents, the children shall become the peculiar care of the community, and proper persons be appointed to take the more immediate charge of them, and as far as possible supply the place of their natural parents.

XXXI. That the Committee of Management shall not be empowered to admit a new member without the consent of three-fourths of the members of the community, obtained at a general meeting.

XXXII. That, although, at the period when all the members shall have been trained and educated under the proposed arrangements, any regulations against misconduct will be unnecessary; and, although it is anticipated that the influence of these new circumstances upon the character of the individuals whose habits and dispositions have been formed under a different system, will be sufficiently powerful to render any serious difference of rare occurrence among them; yet, in order to provide against such, it shall be a law of the community, that, when differences arise, they be referred to the decision of arbitrators, to be elected by the society, who, after hearing the parties, shall decide upon the case.

XXXIII. That if the conduct of any individual be injurious to the well-being of the community, and it be so decided by three-fourths of the members assembled at a general meeting, the committee shall explain to him in what respect his conduct has been injurious, and at the same time intimate to him, that, unless the cause of complaint be removed, they are instructed to expel him from the community.

XXXIV. That any member wishing to withdraw from the community, be at full liberty to do so at any time; and the committee shall be authorized to allow any such gratuity as the circumstances of the case may require.

XXXV. That the committee form arrangements by which all the members shall enjoy equal opportunities of visiting their friends elsewhere, or of travelling for information or other objects.

XXXVI. That the committee appoint duly qualified persons to travel from time to time, to collect scientific and other information for the benefit of the community.

XXXVII. That, in order to extend the benefits of a system of union and co-operation which is applicable to mankind in every part of the world, measures be adopted by the committee to disseminate a knowledge of the new principles and arrangements.

XXXVIII. That, as this system is directly opposed to secrecy and exclusion of any kind, every practicable facility shall be given to strangers, to enable them to become acquainted with the constitution, laws, and regulations of the community, and to examine the results which these have produced in practice.

XXXIX. That the committee be charged with the duty of communicating on all occasions to the Government of the country, an unreserved explanation of the views and proceedings of the community.

ORATION,

Containing A

Declaration of Mental Independence,

Delivered

In the Public Hall, at New Harmony, Ind., by

ROBERT OWEN,

At the Celebration of the Fourth of July,

1826.

ORATION,

We meet to commemorate the period, when the inhabitants of this new world attained the power to withdraw from the control of the old world, and to form a government for themselves.

This event is likely to prove, in its consequences, as important as any which has occurred in ancient or modern times. It has been the means of preparing a new era in the history of man, and of producing such a change of circumstances as will admit of the introduction of measures to change, entirely, the character and condition of the human race.

The revolution in America, sanctioned and secured by the Declaration of Independence in 1776, gave to a people advancing towards civilization, the first opportunity of establishing a government, which would, by degrees, permit them to acquire that greatest of blessings, MENTAL LIBERTY.

This was, indeed, a most important point gained: it was the first time such privilege had been ever possessed by mankind.

Its fruits have been visible in the gradual advance towards mental liberty, which has been made during the half century which this day completes from that memorable event. But, I conclude, it will be in the next half century, now about to commence, that the wondering world will learn justly to estimate the value of the high achievement which was then attained.

It was not the mere political liberty then conquered from the old world, that was the real victory gained by the inhabitants of these vast regions; for political power had been often wrested from one party and obtained by another: But, it was the right which they thereby acquired and used, to establish the liberty of freely extending thought upon all subjects, secular and religious; and the right to express those thoughts openly, so soon as the existing prejudices, derived from the old world, could be so far removed as to direct the mind of the multitude to investigate facts and reject the mysteries of disordered imaginations: to teach them to discern the value of the former, as they always direct to the development of real knowledge; and instruct them rightly to estimate the evil of the latter, as they

67

lead to those errors which have made man a compound of folly and a recipient for misery.

Yes, my friends, the Declaration of Independence, in 1776, prepared the way to secure to you MENTAL LIBERTY, without which man never can become more than a mere localized being, with powers to render him more miserable and degraded than the animals which he has been taught to deem inferior to himself. It is true, the right of mental liberty is inherent in our nature; for, while man exists in mental health, no human power can deprive him of it: but until the Revolution of 1776, no people had acquired the *political power* to permit them to use that right, when their minds should be so far freed from early imbibed prejudices as to allow them to drive benefits from its practice. No nation, except this, even yet possesses the political power to enable the people to use the right of mental freedom.

This right—this invaluable right, you now enjoy by the Constitution obtained for you by Washington, Franklin, Henry, and the other worthies associated with them.

You have indeed abundant reason to rejoice in this victory, obtained over the thick mental darkness which, till then, covered the earth.

The collision of mind which produced that victory, and which was produced by it, elicited a spark of light, which enabled the prominent actors in those scenes to discover a glimpse through the long night of error and misrule, with which the inhabitants of all the earth had been previously afflicted.

Still, however, these men, whose minds were in advance of the age in which they lived, were encircled by the prejudices which they and their fathers brought from Europe, and which had descended to the inhabitants of those regions through many ages of despotism, superstition and ignorance. And although a few of these highly-gifted men of the Revolution saw a stronger and clearer light at the distance, as they supposed, of some ages before them; they were too conscious of the extent of the old errors around them to attempt more than to secure the means in the Constitution which they formed, by which their successors might work their way to the superior distant light, and gain for themselves the innumerable advantages which real mental liberty could bestow upon them.

It is for YOU and YOUR successors now to press onward, with your utmost speed, in the course which, by so many sacrifices, for your benefit, they have opened for you. They discovered some of the

innumerable impositions which had been practised on your predecessors; they saw more of them, than in the temper of those times,
they could venture publicly to expose; but they have left such decided
proofs of their own feelings and views regarding them, that none,
who reflect, can doubt the strong desire they felt to attack and
destroy still more of them, and, if possible, to annihilate all the arts
and mysteries by which the few had so long held a pernicious,
despotic sway and control over the many.

These wise men were withheld from going beyond the line determined upon at the Revolution, apprehending that, by attempting to
gain a greater advance upon ignorance and superstition, they might
put to hazard the benefits they found they could secure; and herein
they evinced their knowledge of the times in which they lived and
acted.

These worthies knew, that their descendants, starting from the
point which they had gained, could, in due time, without such risk,
make other and still more important advances toward mental liberty—
toward that which will, when fully attained, enable man to remove
the cause of all crime, and the misery which arises from the com-
mission of crimes. To attain this mental liberty, in its full extent and
highest purity, and to be secure in its permanent possession, will be
the greatest victory that man can gain.

My friends, it surely cannot be your wish, that any good and great
cause should be effected only by halves,—and more especially when
that which remains to be done, is, beyond all calculation, the more
important? There is a noble object before us, to be won by some
party or another in this or in some other country. It is no less than the
destruction of the threefold causes which deprive man of mental
liberty, which compel him to commit crimes, and to suffer all the
miseries which crime can inflict. Could we but gain this object—soon
would rational intelligence, real virtue, and substantial happiness, be
permanently established among men: ignorance, poverty, dependence,
and vice, would be forever banished from the earth.

Let me now ask,—

Are you prepared to imitate the example of your ancestors? Are
you willing to run the risks which they encountered? Are you ready,
like them, to meet the prejudices of past times, and determined to
overcome them at ALL hazards, for the benefit of your country and
for the emancipation of the human race? Are you, indeed, willing to
sacrifice your fortunes, lives, and reputations, if such sacrifices should

be necessary, to secure for all your fellow-beings, the GREATEST GOOD, that, according to our present knowledge, it is possible for them ever to receive?

Are you prepared to achieve a MENTAL REVOLUTION, as superior in benefit and importance to the first revolution, as the mental powers of man exceed his physical powers?

If you are, I am most ready and willing to join you in this deed— the last and most daring that has been left for man in his irrational state to perform.

But, my friends, knowing, as I do, the immeasurable magnitude of the GOOD which this Mental Revolution will effect and permanently secure for human nature through all future ages—I deem the continued existence, a little longer here, of a few individuals to be of no consideration whatever in comparison with its attainment; and, therefore, as I cannot know the present state of *your* minds, and as the continuance of life at my age, is very uncertain, I have calmly and deliberately determined, upon this eventful and auspicious occasion, to break asunder the remaining mental bonds which for so many ages have grievously afflicted our nature, and, by so doing, to give forever FULL FREEDOM TO THE HUMAN MIND.

Upon an experience, then, of nearly forty years, which owing to a very peculiar combination of circumstances, has been more varied, extended and singular, than perhaps has ever fallen to the lot of any one man, and, during which period, my mind was continually occupied in tracing the cause of each human misery that came before me to its true origin;—I now DECLARE, to you and to the world, *that Man, up to this hour, has been, in all parts of the earth, a slave to a TRINITY of the most monstrous evils that could be combined to inflict mental and physical evil upon his whole race.*

I refer to PRIVATE, OR INDIVIDUAL PROPERTY—ABSURD AND IRRATIONAL SYSTEMS OF RELIGION—AND MARRIAGE, FOUNDED ON INDIVIDUAL PROPERTY COMBINED WITH SOME ONE OF THESE IRRATIONAL SYSTEMS OF RELIGION.

It is difficult to say which of these grand sources of all crime ought to be placed first or last; for they are so intimately interlinked and woven together by time, that they cannot be separated without being destroyed:—each one is necessary to the support of the other two. This formidable Trinity, compounded of Ignorance, Superstition and Hypocrisy, is the only Demon, or Devil, that ever has, or, most likely, ever will torment the human race. It is well calculated, in all its consequences, to produce the utmost misery on the mind and body of man of which his nature is susceptible. The division of property among individuals prepared the seeds, cultivated the growth, and brought to maturity all the evils of poverty and riches existing among a people at the same time; the industrious experiencing privations and the idle being overwhelmed and injured by wealth.

Religion, or Superstition,—for all religions have proved themselves to be Superstitions,—by destroying the judgment, irrationalized all the mental faculties of man, and made him the most abject slave, through the fear of nonentities created solely by his own disordered imagination. Superstition forced him to believe, or to say he believed, that a Being existed who possessed all power, wisdom and goodness—that he could do and that he did, everything—and yet, that evil and misery superabound; and that this Being, who makes and does all things, is not the direct or indirect author of evil or misery. Such is the foundation on which all the mysteries and ravings of Superstition are erected in all parts of the world. Its inconsistency and inconceivable folly have been such as to keep the world in continual wars, and massacres, to create private divisions, leading to every imaginable evil; and it is probable that Superstition has caused more than its third of the crimes and sufferings of the human race.

The forms and ceremonies of Marriage, as they have been hitherto generally performed, and afterwards supported, make it almost certain, that they were contrived and forced upon the people at the same period that property was first divided among a few leading individuals and Superstition was invented: This being the only device that could be introduced to permit them to retain their division of the public spoils, and create to themselves an aristocracy of wealth, of power, and of learning.

To enable them to keep their children apart from the multitude who were to be kept in poverty, in ignorance, and consequently without power,—and to monopolize all wealth and power and learning to themselves,—some such contrivance as Marriage, with mysterious forms and ceremonies, to hide their real intentions from the ignorant, was absolutely necessary, that they might, through the influence of their wealth, learning and power, select the most beautiful and desirable women from among all the people,—and thus enslave and make them, in fact, a part of their private property.

This was the commencement of that system which led to such endless crimes and miseries and degradation of the human faculties, by tempting the inexperienced to barter their feelings and affections for wealth, trappings, and power; when too late for their happiness, they discover they have been deceived, and that wealth, learning and power, can make no amends for the want of those natural feelings and affections, in the union of which, all feel the present happiness of life to consist.

Among the truly intelligent, Marriage will be respected only when it shall be formed between those who are equal in wealth, education and condition; who are well acquainted with each other's habits, minds and feelings, before they enter upon the engagement; and who know also, that by their nature the continuance of affection does not depend upon the will of either, but that it will diminish or increase according as they produce pleasurable or disagreeable sensations in each other. Marriage, to make it a virtuous and happy connexion, must be contracted by both parties, solely with a view to their happiness. As, then, it is a law of nature that our affections are not at the control of the will; and as happiness can be enjoyed only when we associate with those for whom we cannot avoid having the most esteem, regard and affection; it should be as reputable, and equally authorized by law, to dissolve marriage when the esteem and affection cannot be retained for each other, and when the union promises to produce more misery than happiness, as to form the marriage in the first instance. When however the parties are on a perfect equality in wealth, condition and education, and intimately acquainted with each other's thoughts and feelings before marriage; and when no motive whatever exists but genuine affection to induce the parties to unite; it is most likely that marriages so formed would be more permanent than they have ever yet been. But the present and past character of man, formed by the inconsistent and incongruous circumstances around him, have made him so artificial in his feelings, views and conduct, that a decisive conclusion cannot be drawn upon this most interesting part of the subject. Be this, however, as it may, we may be sure, that as soon as man shall be trained rationally, and surrounded by those circumstances only which are in unison with his nature, he will act only rationally; that is, in such a manner as to secure the highest and purest happiness to himself and his fellow-creatures.

The revolution, then, to be now effected, is the DESTRUCTION of this HYDRA OF EVILS—in order that the many may be no longer poor, wretched beings,—dependent on the wealthy and powerful few;

that Man may be no longer a superstitious idiot, continually dying from the futile fear of death; that he may no longer unite himself to the other sex from any mercenary or superstitious motives, nor promise and pretend to do that which it depends not on himself to perform.

Upon the experience of a life devoted to the investigation of these momentous subjects, I fearlessly now declare to you, from a conviction, as strong as conviction can exist in the human mind, that this compound of ignorance and fraud, IS THE REAL AND ONLY CAUSE OF ALL THE CRIME, AND MISERY ARISING FROM CRIME, WHICH CAN BE FOUND IN HUMAN SOCIETY.

This threefold, horrid monster, has been most speciously gilded and decorated with external trappings, to awe the ignorant multitude and deter them from examining the black venom and corruption within. It was in sundry times and places made death for any mortal, except the initiated, to approach these hidden mysteries; and nothing short of the Inquisition with the aid of that fearful unmeaning term SACRED, could have, for so long a period, kept man,—irrational as these terrors made him,—from discovering the imposition which was practised upon him for the sole purpose of keeping him in mental slavery and bondage.

For nearly forty years have I been employed, heart and soul, day by day, almost without ceasing, in preparing the means and arranging the circumstances, to enable me to give the death blow to the tyranny and despotism, which, for unnumbered ages past, have held the human mind spell-bound, in chains and fetters of such mysterious forms and shapes, that no mortal hand dared approach to set the suffering prisoner free. Nor has the fulness of time, for the accomplishment of this great event, been completed until within this hour,— and such has been the extraordinary course of events, that the Declaration of Political Independence, in 1776, has produced its counterpart, the DECLARATION OF MENTAL INDEPENDENCE in 1826—the latter just half a century from the former.

Rejoice with me, my friends, that your Mental Independence rests now as secure as your Political Independence; for the overwhelming power of TRUTH over Error is such, that as soon as arrangements can be formed to admit of the full development of Truth to the world, and it is once publicly promulgated, no art, or falsehood, or force, can ever afterwards return it back into forgetfulness, or unteach the truths which it has taught.

Under the circumstances in which this Mental Revolution has

been made, no human power can undo, or render nugatory, that which has now been done.

This Truth has passed from me, beyond the possibility of recall: it has been already received into your minds: speedily it will be heard throughout America, and from thence it will pass North and South, East and West, as far as language is known,—and almost as fast as it shall be conveyed, human nature will recognize and receive it. In countries, in which ignorance and despotism hold their sway over the multitude, arts will be used to keep it from being heard among them: but neither armies, nor barriers of any kind, can now prevent a great and important truth from finding its way, by some means or another, into the darkest recesses of error and deception.

Rejoice, then, with me, my friends, that this light is now set upon a hill; for it will increase daily, more and more, until it shall be seen, felt, and understood, by all the nations of the earth.

Rejoice, with me, that we now live under a government unconnected with any of the supersitions of the dark ages of ignorance; a government established purposely to give man his natural rights; to give him the full power to obtain mental liberty as soon as he could disburthen himself of the prejudices of his ancestors.

The individuals who compose a great majority of your present general government are happily free from the weakening and deadening influence of Superstition; their experience is too extensive, their minds are too enlightened, to be longer held in slavery and bondage by imaginary notions unsupported by a single fact. They will therefore rejoice to see their fellow-citizens and their fellow-men throwing off the yoke which has hitherto kept their finest faculties in bondage, and they will look forward with increased hope to the advantages which the rising generation, freed from these errors, will acquire and possess.

All who are deeply versant in human nature can readily estimate the difference between a generation, whose judgment shall have been carefully cultivated from infancy, and whose best faculties shall have been early called into full action, and one in which the judgment has been forced to become subservient to a misguided imagination, and in whose mind all natural facts have been distorted and made to bend and support mysteries only calculated to blind the understanding and call forth the weaker and worse feelings of human nature. Your government, and all the enlightened men of these States and of other countries, now look to the improved education of the faculties of children, to produce a race of rational beings, whose minds will be freed from the superstitions, prejudices, and errors of past times; and I trust, that in this respect, no parties will be disappointed.

In furtherance of this great object we are preparing the means to bring up your children, with industrious and useful habits, with natural, and of course rational ideas and views, with sincerity in all their proceedings; and to give them kind and affectionate feelings for each other, and charity, in the most extensive sense of the term, for all their fellow-creatures.

By doing this, by uniting your separate interests into one, by doing away with individual money transactions, by exchanging with each other your articles of produce on the basis of labor for equal labor, by looking forward to apply your surplus wealth to assist others to obtain similar advantages, and by the abandonment of the use of spirituous liquors, you will in a peculiar manner promote the object of every wise government and of all really enlightened men.

And here we now are, as near, perhaps, as we can be in the center of the United States, even, as it were, like the little grain of mustard seed; but with these GREAT TRUTHS before us, with the practice of the social system, as soon as it shall be well understood among us, our principles will, I trust, spread from Community to Community, from State to State, and from Continent to Continent, until this System and these TRUTHS shall overshadow the whole earth,— shedding fragrance and abundance, intelligence and happiness, upon all the sons of men.

I would that you, and those who now live in this and other countries, could partake, for many years, of all these enjoyments.

A WORKING BIBLIOGRAPHY

I. Major Works by Robert Owen

The list given here is substantially that provided on pages 10 and 11 of A. L. Morton's *Life and Ideas of Robert Owen*, expanded only by the addition of the three speeches published herewith, and by the "Appeal to the Capitalists and Men of Extensive Practical Experience in New York" which was reprinted in Vol. VII of Commons' *Documentary History of American Industrial Society*. The titles are arranged in chronological order.

❖   ❖   ❖   ❖   ❖

A New View of Society: or Essays on the Principles of the Formation of Human Character, 1813.
Observations on the Effect of the Manufacturing System, 1815.
An Address to the Inhabitants of New Lanark, 1816.
Report to the Committee for the Relief of the Manufacturing Poor, 1817.
A Catechism of the New View of Society and Three Addresses, 1817.
Further Development of the Plan for the Relief of the Poor and the Emancipation of Mankind, 1817.
On the Employment of Children in Manufactories, 1818.
To the British Master Manufacturers, 1818.
An Address to the Working Classes, 1819.
Report to the County of Lanark, 1821.
Address to the Congress of the United States, Feb. 25, 1825.
Second Address to the Congress of the United States, March 7, 1825.
Oration on the Fourth of July, New Harmony, Indiana, July 4, 1826.
An Appeal to the Rich, 1833 (This appears on page 149 of Morton's *Life and Ideas of Robert Owen,* quoted from Bronterre O'Brien's translation (1836) of *Buonarroti's History of Babeuf's Conspiracy for Equality.*)
A Dialogue in Three Parts, between the Founder of "The Association of All Classes of All Nations," and a Stranger, 1838.
An Address to All Classes, Sects and Parties, 1840.
Lectures on the Marriages of the Priesthood of the Old Immoral World. 4th ed. with an Appendix. 1841.
An Appeal to Capitalists and Men of Extensive Practical Experience in New York, 1845. Quoted in Vol. VII, p. 166, of *The Documentary History of American Industrial Society,* edited by J. R. Commons.
The Revolution in the Mind and Practice of the Human Race, 1849.
Robert Owen's Millennial Gazette, No. 11, Aug. 1, 1857.
The Life of Robert Owen by Himself, 1857. Reprinted by G. Bell, London, 1920.

A Supplementary Appendix to the First Volume of the Life of Robert Owen, 1858.

✿   ✿   ✿   ✿   ✿

II. Works About Robert Owen, or Referring Significantly to Him

The following list does not pretend to be exhaustive. The emphasis is on works published in the United States, designed to indicate the extent of American interest in Owen, and the American share in world Owenite scholarship.

✿   ✿   ✿   ✿   ✿

ALLABONE, S. AUSTIN, *Allabone's Dictionary of Authors*: A Critical Dictionary of English Literature and British and American Authors, Living and Deceased, From the Earliest Accounts to the Latter Half of the Nineteenth Century. Philadelphia and London, 1902. (First American copyright is stated to be 1870.) Vol. II, p. 1478. Biographical Sketch of Owen.

ANONYMOUS, "New Harmony," *Weekly People,* New York. April 18, 1964. (Also letter commenting on this article, *Weekly People,* August 8, 1964.)

BESTOR, ARTHUR EUGENE, JR., *Backwoods Utopias.* University of Pennsylvania Press. Philadelphia. 1950. Most complete American study of Robert Owen.

BLAU, LEON JOSEPH, *Social Theories of Jacksonian Democracy,* a documentary collection edited by Joseph L. Blau. Hafner Publishing Co., New York. 1947. Contains some references to Owen; useful for background.

CALVERTON, V. F. (pseudonym of George Goetz), *Where Angels Dared to Tread.* Bobbs-Merrill Co., Indianapolis and New York. 1941. Quotes from Owen's later writings: "I had hoped that fifty years of political liberty had prepared the American people to govern themselves advantageously. . . . But now upon my return I find that the habits of the individual system were so powerful that these leases [of property] have been, with a few exceptions, applied for individual purposes and individual gain."

CLEMENT, M. HENRY, "Histoire d'un Reformateur," *Reforme Sociale* (now *Les Etudes Sociales*), Serie 8, tome 2 (tome 72), 1916, pp. 147-175.

COLE, G. D. H., "Owen and Owenism," *Encyclopedia of the Social Sciences,* Macmillan, New York, 1942. Vol. 11-12, pp. 518-520. Discusses Owenism in relation to Marxism (in the final paragraphs), especially in educational and philosophical theory.

———— *Life of Robert Owen,* 3rd edition, Shoestring Press, New York, 1966.

COMMONS, J. R., and Associates, editors, *Documentary History of American Industrial Society.* Macmillan. New York. Vol. V, edited by Professor Commons and Helen Sumner, gives much attention to Robert Dale Owen; Vol. VII, edited by Professor Commons, quotes in full several of Owen's articles that appeared in the American press while he was in this country.

DEBORIN, A. M., "The Teaching of Robert Owen." In the volume, *The History of the Working Class and Revolutionary Movement*. Moscow, 1958, pp. 605-628.

———— "The Utopian Communism of Robert Owen and the Chartist Movement." Included in *Research in the History of World Culture*. Moscow, 1959. No. 6, pp. 3-16.

ELY, PROF. R. T., *The Labor Movement in America*. New York. 1886.

EMERSON, RALPH WALDO, *Complete Works*, edited by Edward Waldo Emerson. Houghton, Mifflin Co. Boston & New York. 1903-1932. Vol. X, pp. 346-347; and Notes, pp. 578-579.

ENGELS, FREDERICK, *Anti-Dühring*. International Publishers. New York. 1934.

ESTABROOK, ARTHUR H., "The Family History of Robert Owen," *Indiana Magazine of History*, Vol. XIX, No. 1, pp. 63-101, March, 1923. Gives interesting details about the individual members of Owen's family, including Mrs. Owen's ancestry.

FROW, E., "Robert Owen," *Marxism Today*, London, October, 1958, pp. 296-300. Makes use of recent British research into the contemporary literature of Owen's day, with emphasis on the Chartists.

GORB, PETER, "Robert Owen as a Businessman." *Bulletin* of the Business Historical Society, Vol. XXV (Sept., 1951), No. 3, pp. 127-148. Poses the question of *what* caused the "change of direction of his interest," i.e., from profit-making to social reform.

GOULD, KENNETH M., "Robert Owen: Backwater of History?" *The American Scholar*, Spring, 1938. Vol. 7, No. 2, pp. 153-170. Says that "a rehearsal of his [Owen's] contributions has definite value today for all who are concerned with the embryology of the future social order."

GRANT, BETTY, "Robert Owen and Co-operative Production," *Marxism Today*, London, November, 1958, pp. 333-338. Studies the inter-relationships between the Owenites, the Chartists, and the Christian Socialists.

HARRISON, JOHN F. C., *Utopianism and Education: Robert Owen and the Owenites*. Teachers College Columbia University. New York. 1969. A collection of essays, with the Editor's Introduction: Four by Robert Owen, one by Robert Dale Owen, one by Jane Dale Owen, and one each by three "Owenites"—Abram Combe, William Thompson, and William Maclure. Professor Harrison gives new emphasis to Owen's contribution to pedagogy.

HARVEY, ROWLAND HILL, *Robert Owen: Social Idealist*. University of California Publications in History. Berkeley and Los Angeles. Vol. 38, 1949. Calls attention to a controversy between Owen and Malthus. "Malthus did indeed," says Harvey, "prove a strong fortress for the conscience of the rich. Behind the great walls of his arguments the calloused hid, deaf to the cries of the hungry."

HILLQUIT, MORRIS, *History of Socialism in the United States*. Funk & Wagnalls Co. New York & London. 1903. Summarizes the Noyes work, then describes Socialism from then on as a political, not a communitarian, movement.

HIMES, NORMAN E., "Robert Dale Owen," Encyclopedia of the Social
    Sciences, Macmillan, New York, 1942. Vol. 11-12, pp. 517-518.
    Says Robert Dale Owen "led a successful fight for a bill securing
    property rights for women," in the Indiana legislature. Also says:
    "At a strategic moment he helped crystallize Lincoln's views on
    slavery."

HUBBARD, ELBERT, "Robert Owen." Little Journeys, Vol. 24, No. 1, 1919.

IRVIN, MARY LOUISE, Contemporary American Opinion of the New Harmony
    Movement. Master's Thesis. University of Illinois, 1932. Unpublished.

JEFFERSON, THOMAS, The Writings of Thomas Jefferson, edited by Paul
    Leicester Ford. G. P. Putnam's Sons. New York. 1892-1899. Vol. X,
    p. 344.

JOHNSON, OAKLEY C., "Robert Owen: Genius and Socialist Pioneer," an
    article commemmorating the 100th anniversary of Owen's death.
    The Worker. New York. Nov. 23, 1958.

———— "Portrait of a Great Utopian." Political Affairs. February, 1964,
    p. 60. (Book review.)

———— "Education in Utopia," World Magazine, May 3, 1969, p. M-11.
    (Book Review.)

JORDAN, DAVID STARR, and AMOS W. BUTLER, "New Harmony," Scientific
    Monthly, XXV (November, 1927), pp. 468-470. This was reprinted
    from Proceedings, Centennial Anniversary of Western Science, May
    12-14, 1927; and again reprinted in Proceedings, Indiana Academy
    of Science, XXXVII, pp. 59-62, 1928.

KAN, S. B., History of Socialistic Ideas. (Before the creation of Marxism.)
    A Course of Lectures. Moscow. The Higher School Publishing House.
    1963. For Robert Owen, see pp. 146-171.

KARATAYEV, N. K., editor. History of Economic Theory. (Manual for
    Economic Colleges.) State Socio-Economic Publishing House. Mos-
    cow. 1963. For Robert Owen, see pp. 101-103.

KARATAYEV, N. K. and STEPANOV, I. G., History of Economic Theories of
    Western Europe and Russia. (Before the creation of Marxism.) A
    Course of Lectures. State Socio-Economic Publishing House. 1959.
    For Robert Owen, see pp. 278-307.

KOROVIN, K. S., Predecessors of Scientific Socialism on the Subject of a Just
    Distribution of Products in Society. Publications of the Leningrad
    Institute of Economics and Engineering. 1961. Vol. 35.
    For Robert Owen, see pp. 151-152, and other references.

LEIBOWITZ, IRVING, My Indiana. Prentice-Hall, Inc. Englewood Cliffs, N. J.
    1964. Chapter XII, "The Dreamers," deals with the Robert Owen
    family.

LOCKWOOD, GEORGE BROWNING, The New Harmony Movement. With the
    collaboration of Charles A. Prosser on the educational chapters.
    D. Appleton & Co. New York. 1905. The Introduction is by W. T.
    Harris, United States Commissioner of Education.

MADISON, CHARLES A., Critics and Crusaders: A Century of American
    Protest. Henry Holt & Co. New York. 1946. Contains a selection on
    "The Utopians," pp. 83-93.

MARX & ENGELS, *Selected Works*, Vols. I and II. Moscow. 1962. Contains some twenty specific references in the two volumes, with extensive discussion.

MAYER, GUSTAV, *Friedrich Engels: A Biography*. A. A. Knopf. New York. 1936.

MCMASTER, JOHN BACH, A *History of the People of the United States*. New York. 1910. Vol. V, pp. 88-108. Implies that New Harmony was successful only when Robert Owen himself was on the scene. "Idleness and waste gave place to industry and thrift such as had not been seen since the Rappites left New Harmony." Also deals in detail with the work of Frances Wright and Robert Dale Owen, and how the working class supported the social reforms they led—free public school, abolition of imprisonment for debt, equal rights for women, the eight-hour day, etc.

MEHRING, FRANZ, *Karl Marx: The Story of His Life*. Covici, Friede, Inc. New York. 1935.

MORTON, A. L., *The Life and Ideas of Robert Owen*. Monthly Review Press. New York. 1963. (A publisher's note states that this work originally appeared in France, then in England.) Perhaps the best short all-round exposition.

———— "Utopia as a Reflection of Social Ideas." *Marxism Today*, November, 1962, p. 336 ff. Discusses utopian writers from More to Huxley, including the Americans, Edward Bellamy, Jack London, and Ignatius Donnelly.

———— "The Rediscovery of Chartism," *Marxism Today*, March, 1960, p. 83f, and "The Interpretation of Chartism," *Marxism Today*, June, 1961, p. 177f. These articles put Chartism (and, incidentally, Owenism) into pre-Marxist perspective.

NATIONAL LIBRARY OF WALES, THE, A *Bibliography of Robert Owen, The Socialist, 1771-1858*. Aberystwyth, Wales, 1914. Originally 54 pages, and expanded in 1925 to 90 pages; shows pride in a native son's achievements.

NIEUWENHUIS, F. DOMELA, "Robert Owen éducateur." *La Societe Nouvelle: Revue internationale Sociologie, Arts, Sciences, Letters*. 15me Année — Tome IV, p. 5-17. (2me Série — Vol. XXXVI). Avril — Mai — Juin, 1910. Paris. Emphasizes Owen's educational achievements, and brackets Owen and Fourier as pedagogical innovators.

NOVIKOV, V. A., "Utopian Socialism in Western Europe." (A Lecture.) Moscow. Publication of the Higher Party School, Academy of Social Sciences, 1961. (Higher Party School of the Central Committee of the Communist Party of the Soviet Union, Department of Political Economy.) Pp. 21-23, and other references.

NOYES, JOHN HUMPHREY, *History of American Socialisms*. Philadelphia, 1870. First comprehensive historical survey of socialist experiments in the United States.

OWEN, ROBERT DALE, *Threading My Way*, an autobiography by the oldest son of Robert Owen. New York. 1874.

PACKARD, FREDERIC ADOLPHUS, *Life of Robert Owen.* Ashmead and Evans, Philadelphia. 1866. The Preface says: "There are thousands of minds in our country exercised on the subject of social evils and their remedy."

PARRINGTON, VERNON L., JR., *American Dreams: A Study of American Utopias.* Providence, R. I. 1947. Contains detail on a relatively large number of earlier American utopian novelists.

PODMORE, FRANK, *Robert Owen: A Biography.* Two vols. D. Appleton & Co. First published in London, 1906; first American publication, 1907. Re-issued in 1924. Contains 14 portraits of Owen. Author Eugene Bestor, Jr., calls this "the standard biography of Robert Owen."

POKROVSKY, V. S., "Socio-political Opinions of the Utopian Socialists of the First Half of the 19th Century." (A Lecture.) Moscow. 1953. State Evening Juridical Institute.
For Robert Owen, see pp. 43-58.

REINDERS, ROBERT C., "T. Wharton Collens and the Christian Labor Union," *Labor History,* Winter, 1967, Vol. VIII. Traces the career of a New Orleans Catholic layman who was influenced by Owen's economic views.

REUEL, A. L., *West European Utopian Socialism.* (A Textbook.) Moscow, 1963. Moscow Financial Institute.
For Robert Owen, see pp. 53-69, and other references.

STRACHEY, JOHN, *The Theory and Practice of Socialism.* Random House, New York. 1936. Chapter XXIV, "Robert Owen and the Communist Colonies," pp. 299-317. Notable for bringing in the name of William Morris in the discussion of Robert Owen. Strachey writes: "Thirty-three years after his [Owen's] death, the poet and socialist, William Morris, published *News from Nowhere.*" But Morris, says Strachey, had what Owen lacked—a knowledge of scientific socialism, and of *how* socialism could actually get started.

TAGIEV, A. M., *The Pedagogical Views of Robert Owen (1771-1858.)* A Manual for the Students of the State Correspondence Pedagogical Institute of Azerbaijan. Baku. 1958. (15 pp.) This manual is in the Azerbaijanian language.

TAWNEY, R. H., *The Radical Tradition,* edited by Rita Hinden. Geo. Allen & Unwin, Ltd., London, 1964. "Robert Owen," pp. 32-39. Tells why Owen went to America.

THOMPSON, E. P., *The Making of the English Working Class.* Penguin Books, Ltd., 1963, and Pelican Books, 1968, Oxford, England. See "Owenism," pages 857-887. Owen's work is placed in a 300-year historical panorama, and in this sense the whole work is relevant to Owen.

TIMMONS, WILBERT, "Robert Owen's Texas Project," *The Southwestern Historical Quarterly,* Vol. LII, No. 3, pp. 286-293. January, 1949. Timmons, like Reinders, reveals Owen's Southern influence in this country.

TUMIN-ALMEDINGEN, N. A., *The Pedagogical Experiments and Principles of Robert Owen.* Edited by Gollant, E. Y. Moscow. Pedagogical State Publishing House. 1960. 164 pp. (Bibliography, pp. 161-163.)

UDALL, STEWART L., *Remarks* by Secretary of the Interior Stewart L. Udall at Presentation of National Landmark Plaque, New Harmony, Indiana, August 21, 1965. Press Release by the United States Department of the Interior, Washington, D.C., August 21, 1965. Speaks of "New Harmony on the honor roll of the Registered National Historic Landmarks," and refers to "the heritage which has been handed to us from cities like New Harmony, and leaders like Robert Owen."

UDALTZOV, I. D., and POLYANSKY, F. Y. *History of Economic Theory.* (A Course of Lectures.) Part I. Published by Moscow University. 1961. For Robert Owen, see pp. 484-497.

VOLGIN, V. P., "Robert Owen," Introduction to the *Selected Works of Robert Owen.* Moscow and Leningrad, 1950, pp. 5-64.

VOZNESENSKAYA, V. A., *Economic Ideas of the Great Socialist Utopians of the West.* Moscow. State Socio-Economic Publishing House. 1958.

WILSON, WILLIAM E., *The Angel and the Serpent: The Story of New Harmony.* Indiana University Press. Bloomington. 1964. Good for its emphasis on local aspects of Owenite history. Marred by an over-hasty generalization about Owen's attitude toward Negroes.

WOLINS, LEROY, "The 150th Anniversary of New Harmony," *The Worker,* New York. July 12, 1964.

YOUNG, MARGUERITE, *Angel in the Forest*: A Fairy Tale of Two Utopias. Reynall & Hitchcock, New York, 1945. (Reprinted by Scribner's in 1966.) "Who fails to love this man fails to love humanity," says Miss Young of Robert Owen, in this poetic and witty book.

ZARRIN, P. I., editor, *History of Economic Teachings.* (A Course of Lectures; a textbook for colleges and faculties of economics.) Moscow. The Higher School Publishing House. 1963. For Robert Owen, see pp. 185-193.

ZIKEEVA, O. N., "Labor Education in the Communist Communities of Robert Owen." *Soviet Pedagogy.* 1959. No. 5, pp. 79-89. (The Bibliography contains 14 titles.)

INDEX